The Critical Idiom
Founder Editor: John D. Jump, 1969-76

36   *Dramatic Monologue*

Dramatic Monologue

Alan Sinfield

Methuen & Co Ltd : London
Barnes & Noble Books : New York

First published 1977
by Methuen & Co Ltd
11 New Fetter Lane London EC4P 4EE
© 1977 Alan Sinfield

Typeset by Inforum Ltd., Portsmouth
and printed in Great Britain by
J.W. Arrowsmith Ltd., Bristol 3

ISBN 0 416 70540 5 (Hardback)
ISBN 0 416 70630 4 (Paperback)

Distributed in the USA by
HARPER & ROW PUBLISHERS INC
BARNES & NOBLE IMPORT DIVISION

Contents

Preface

Dramatic monologue, like several other topics in the *Critical Idiom* series, is both a poetic form with certain properties and the favoured mode of a particular literary period (about 1830-1930). Part of my theme is that dramatic monologue is not confined to one century, and the first half of the book is about its potential as a form, working roughly from simpler aspects to the more complex. The second half is chronologically organized and seeks to explain why the Victorians developed the naturalistic monologue and relied so heavily upon it, how Pound and Eliot changed it and why it returned to occasional use.

It is a pleasure to express my gratitude to friends and colleagues who by commenting on drafts of this book or discussing it with me helped to make the writing of it a stimulating experience: Peter Nicholls, Patricia Thomson, Manfred Pfister, John Gingell, Martin Monks.

Alan Sinfield

Acknowledgements

The author and publishers would like to thank the following for permission to reprint the extracts from poems given in the book:

Faber and Faber for lines from 'Histrion' (in Ezra Pound's *A Lume Spento*), 'Villonaud for this Yule', 'Cino' and 'The River Merchant's Wife' (in Ezra Pound's *Collected Shorter Poems*), 'Journey of the Magi' and 'Little Gidding' (in T.S. Eliot's *Collected Poems 1909-1962*); Faber and Faber and Robert Lowell for lines from 'Mr Edwards and the Spider' and 'Mother Marie Therese' (in Robert Lowell's *Poems 1938-1949*); Faber and Faber and Ted Hughes for lines from 'Hawk Roosting' (in Ted Hughes' *Lupercal*); The Marvell Press and Philip Larkin for lines from 'Wedding Wind' (in Philip Larkin's *The North Ship*); M.B. Yeats, Miss Anne Yeats and The Macmillan Co of London and Basingstoke for lines from 'The Lamentations of the Old Pensioner' (in W.B. Yeats' *Collected Poems*).

I

Two poems by Browning

An anonymous reviewer of Browning's volume *Men and Women* (1855) wondered:

> Why one who can pour out his thoughts, fancies, stores of learning, and emotions, with an eloquence and direct sincerity such as this, should, so often as Mr Browning has here done, prefer to rhyme the pleadings of a casuist, or the arguments of a critic, or the ponderous discoursings of some obsolete schoolman - why he should turn away from themes in which every one can answer to his sympathies, and from modes of the lyre which find their echoes wherever hearts and ears know aught of music - is an enigma no less painful than perplexing, the unriddling of which is possibly reserved for no contemporary.
>
> (*Browning, The Critical Heritage*, p. 157)

The reviewer had in mind poems like 'My Last Duchess', 'The Bishop Orders his Tomb at St Praxed's Church', 'Andrea del Sarto', 'Fra Lippo Lippi' and 'Bishop Blougram's Apology', where there is a first-person speaker who is not the poet. He is set in a specific situation on a particular occasion; he alone speaks, but partly in response to a silent auditor.

'Fra Lippo Lippi' begins thus:

> I am poor brother Lippo, by your leave!
> You need not clap your torches to my face.
> Zooks, what's to blame? you think you see a monk!
> What, it's past midnight, and you go the rounds,
> And here you catch me at an alley's end
> Where sportive ladies leave their doors ajar.

It is a tense moment because the watch are supposed to arrest
monks found out of their cloisters at night, but they are impressed
when Lippi says he is a painter in the household of Cosimo de'
Medici. He chatters on exuberantly about how he was tempted by
a jovial carnival party to clamber from his window, but sensing
some disapproval explains that he was drawn by poverty into the
monastery as a child. His talent as a painter made him appreciated but he is no saint; indeed, it is the faces and bodies of people
in their marvellous variety which delight him, though the Prior
tells him 'to paint the souls of men'. But God made the world:

> - For what? do you feel thankful, ay or no,
> For this fair town's face, yonder river's line,
> The mountain round it and the sky above,
> Much more the figures of man, woman, child,
> These are the frame to? What's it all about?
> To be passed o'er, despised? or dwelt upon,
> Wondered at? oh, this last of course, you say.

By his painting, he declares, he may 'Interpret God to all of you!'
Yet he goes too far in his enthusiasm and independence from
church orthodoxy and has once more to draw back:

> - That is - you'll not mistake an idle word
> Spoke in a huff by a poor monk, God wot,
> Tasting the air this spicy night which turns
> The unaccustomed head like Chianti wine!
> Oh, the church knows! don't misreport me, now!

To regain his audience he describes a picture he proposes to paint
of God amidst the blessed:

> up shall come
> Out of a corner when you least expect,
> As one by a dark stair into a great light,
> Music and talking, who but Lippo! I! -
> Mazed, motionless and moon-struck - I'm the man!

- and he will be welcomed into heaven by 'a sweet angelic slip of a thing'. The poem ends when Lippi shakes hands and scuttles back to his room.

I have begun with a bemused critic of Browning and 'Fra Lippo Lippi' because Browning is the most celebrated writer of dramatic monologues and this is one of his most celebrated poems, and because perplexity and discouragement is still sometimes the main critical response. In a book such as this it would no doubt be helpful to start with a definition of the form, but there is no generally agreed approach. Two main alternatives appear: to start from 'Fra Lippo Lippi' and Browning's other famous poems and construct a genre which will hold just those few instances; and to postulate a wide category within which Browning's poems are special cases. Most criticism has done the former, and that is the policy we will pursue in the present chapter.

If we are to define dramatic monologue as 'poems like "Fra Lippo Lippi"' then we may add to the properties already remarked - a first-person speaker not the poet, a time and place, an auditor - revelation of character, colloquial language and some dramatic interaction between speaker and auditor. It may then seem that dramatic monologue is a truncated play. If the principal elements of drama are, as Aristotle said, plot and character, then dramatic monologue has very little plot and only one real character. Hence we may conclude that it is a substitute for playwriting for those who have little skill with plot; or, more generously, that it is a kind of drama specially suited to those whose main interest is in character.

'Fra Lippo Lippi' is plainly designed at least in part to display character. The first-person presentation focuses attention upon Lippi, who is made to reveal himself directly through his own speech. The poet does not intervene explicitly to direct our judgment; we experience the richness of human life almost with the impact of a personal encounter. Notice also that the situation and auditor Browning provides place Lippi upon the defensive: his words are influenced by an external pressure so that we see two sides of him, as it were, interacting. Lippi as he thinks of himself and as he is obliged to justify himself in his society are both aspects of the man and each is in part a compromise with the other. We may add to our list of properties, therefore, the notions that the poet does not take a direct role and that the revelation of character is to some extent unwitting. We understand more about the speaker than he intends to reveal to his auditor and than the poet actually states.

We may take another instance, 'My Last Duchess'. Browning's speaker in this poem is an Italian Renaissance duke; he displays a picture of his 'last Duchess'. She seems to have been a charmingly unaffected lady, gracious to rich and poor alike, but the Duke was not satisfied:

> She thanked men, - good; but thanked
> Somehow ... I know not how ... as if she ranked
> My gift of a nine hundred years old name
> With anybody's gift.

He adds the sinister comment,

> This grew; I gave commands;
> Then all smiles stopped together. There she stands
> As if alive.

The implication is that if he did not kill her he contributed, perhaps by his unpleasantness, to her death. It is at this point that we realize that he is speaking to the envoy of the count whose daughter is to be his next wife:

> The Count your Master's known munificence
> Is ample warrant that no just pretence
> Of mine for dowry will be disallowed;
> Though his fair daughter's self, as I avowed
> At starting, is my object.

(Notice the ambiguity of 'object'.) And finally, as they descend the stairs, he points out a statue of Neptune 'Taming a sea-horse ... Which Claus of Innsbruck cast in bronze for me'.

The Duke is obviously a far less appealing figure than Lippi. His egotism demands that he be the focus of all attention. He is happiest with the Duchess when she is trapped in a painting - and even then no one else is normally allowed to look at it - like the statue of Neptune which was made 'for me'. Again the speaker reveals more about himself than he imagines. He says of the Duchess,

> My favour at her breast,
> The dropping of the daylight in the West,
> The bough of cherries some officious fool
> Broke in the orchard for her, the white mule
> She rode with round the terrace - all and each
> Would draw from her alike the approving speech,
> Or blush, at least.

The evocative natural imagery allows the reader to infer the pleasant nature of the Duchess. It is communicated through the Duke's words, but he is quite unable to appreciate it.

We also ask ourselves why the Duke tells all this to the envoy. Will it not deter the next match? Critics disagree: some think the Duke is so self-possessed that he doesn't care what anyone thinks, some that he intends a warning to the next duchess. I see him as less in control. He seems to believe that his egotism manifests his great nobility: he asks, 'Who'd stoop to blame/This sort of trifling?' But he does stoop, he is so petty-minded that he cannot stand it when his wife smiles at a servant. I would argue that his meditation runs on further than he had intended. He is still obsessed with the remarkable girl he failed to dominate, and impelled to justify to himself and others his ruthless response.

The possibility of such varying interpretations of the Duke's words, and the fact that in any event he is hardly attractive, illustrate more fully than 'Fra Lippo Lippi' the effects of the poet's withdrawal from explicit comment on his creations.

One consequence of the poet's reticence is that we are obliged to give consideration to attitudes which in other circumstances we would find repellent. The first-person mode of the poem means that we have no way of understanding what is happening without passing through the Duke's perception of it and thus, temporarily at least, sharing his approach. It is difficult for the reader or audience in a play or novel to resist altogether the point of view of the character through whose perceptions an action is mediated or whose mind is most fully revealed. That is why we feel with Shakespeare's Richard III and Macbeth. In dramatic monologue this effect reaches its strongest form. To comprehend even the simplest factors of time and place we must look through the speaker's eyes and enter his mind, and this requires an exercise of sympathy which influences our attitude to him. 'Look at it this way', we say when trying to persuade someone, and that is the strategy of dramatic monologue.

In his book *The Poetry of Experience* (ch. 2) Robert Langbaum stresses the sympathetic draw of the first person and contends further that it inhibits the reader's judgment of the speaker. This has not been generally accepted, for most commentators find that although we must initially involve ourselves with the Duke, this does not prevent us ultimately from disapproving of him. It may well be that the more we understand him the less we like him.

Indeed, a second consequence of the poet's withdrawal from explicit judgment is that we are stimulated to infer his opinions obliquely from details of the presentation. We intuit Browning's attitude to the Duke from nuances like the imagery of sunset and a bough of cherries which suggest that the Duchess was a delightful person; from the remark about 'stooping' which invites us to consider whether the Duke is as exalted as he claims; and from the final mention of Neptune and the sea-horse which confirms the Duke's egocentricity (it was made 'for me'), his cruelty (the sea-horse is analogous to the Duchess) and his inhumanity (in making the Duchess just one of his collection of objects). Yet we cannot be sure that we have the exclusive interpretation. Judgment is not blocked but is indirect and depends upon our individual reading. 'My Last Duchess' is continuously and radically ironic, for every line consists simultaneously of the Duke's statements and Browning's implications which we must work to realize in ourselves.

A definition of dramatic monologue constructed from these two poems, then, should include a first-person speaker who is not the poet and whose character is unwittingly revealed, an auditor whose influence is felt in the poem, a specific time and place, colloquial language, some sympathetic involvement with the speaker, and an ironic discrepancy between the speaker's view of himself and a larger judgment which the poet implies and the reader must develop.

2

A broader view

The definition reached at the end of the previous chapter has several disadvantages. It is cumbersome; it will serve for only a few poems; and it is not likely that a description of the properties of one or two poems, even though they may be superlative instances, will give us the perspective from which to analyse the essential qualities of the form. Moreover, the definition is undermined already by important differences of emphasis in the poems. Lippi is a naturally sympathetic figure and we enjoy making his acquaintance, whereas the Duke is selfish and cruel and attracts only the temporary involvement needed to understand the poem; he is far more ironically perceived. The roles of the auditors differ. The envoy in 'My Last Duchess' does not, like the watch, affect materially what the speaker says; rather, his mere presence makes us wonder that the Duke is prepared to speak thus before him. And 'Fra Lippo Lippi' is much the more colloquial and dramatic poem. If we bring into consideration other monologues by Browning, let alone Tennyson, the position becomes even less satisfactory.

Such a tight definition of the form helps to describe those two poems but affords little basis for a general understanding of the mode of such poems and their historical significance. In this chapter, therefore, I mean to take the opposite approach, starting from the broadest definition of dramatic monologue as simply a poem in the first person spoken by, or almost entirely by, someone who is indicated not to be the poet. This is what Browning had in mind when he said that many of his poems 'are called "Dramatic" because the story is told by some actor in it, not by the poet

himself' (*The Athenaeum*, January 1890). Such a broad approach
will admit to consideration very many poems which do not satisfy
all the criteria in the constricting definition but which, in my view,
have a good deal in common with Browning's poems. I mean to
look now at some of these examples and thus to open out the conception of what dramatic monologue, broadly defined, may
achieve - though my full analysis is reserved for the next chapter.
We will find that the use of a speaker other than the poet can produce a range of effects and that the specification developed in the
previous chapter represents only one set of possibilities.

We may begin by insisting that the Victorians did not invent the
dramatic monologue of unwitting character revelation by a first-
person speaker without the poet's direct intervention. Rochester
gives us an example in 'A Very Heroical Epistle from my Lord All-
pride to *Doll-Common*' (1679; also called 'A very Heroical
Epistle in Answer to Ophelia') - it will be appreciated that with the
present broad definition the 'speaker' of dramatic monologue
may as well be a writer. Rochester explained, 'Doll-Common
being forsaken by my *Lord-All Pride* and having written him a
most lamentable Letter, his Lordship sends her the following
answer'. It begins,

> Madam,
> If your deceiv'd, it is not by my Cheat,
> For all disguises, are below the Great.
> What *Man*, or *Woman,* upon *Earth* can say,
> I ever us'd 'em well above a Day?
> How is it then, that I inconstant am?
> He changes not, who always is the same.

Lord All-Pride is as pleased with himself as Browning's Duke and
means to impress his reader, but we are likely to see in his attitude
vanity - 'What e're you gave, I paid you back in Bliss' - and brutal
cynicism - women, like beggars, 'still haunt the Door,/ Where
they've receiv'd a *Charity* before'. His hero is the Turkish sultan:

> O happy *Sultan*! whom we barb'rous call,
> How much refin'd art thou above us all:

> Who envys not the joys of thy *Serail?*
> Thee like some God! the trembling Crowd adore,
> Each Man's thy *Slave, Woman kind,* thy *Whore.*

Lord All-Pride's stance is so credibly sustained that the reader who is disinclined to believe that a seventeenth-century poet may invite so indirect a judgment may suspect that this is straightforward, immoral Restoration wit, but our dislike of the speaker is ratified by external evidence: 'All-Pride' was Rochester's nickname for his enemy the Earl of Mulgrave (so was 'Bajazet' and hence, partly, the sultan). At the end of the poem the self-styled great man reveals his petty cowardice: 'Thou fear'st no injur'd *Kinsmans* threatning Blade,/Nor Mid-night Ambushes, by *Rivals* laid'.

Swift also is ironic, though more tolerant and amused, in 'Mrs Harris' Petition to the Lord Justices of Ireland', which he wrote in 1701 in response to an actual event. A servingwoman who has lost her purse rambles over all the circumstances, including how she approached the wife of one of the footmen who she dreamt had it in her trunk:

> However, I was resolv'd to bring the Discourse slily about,
> Mrs *Dukes*, said I, here's an ugly Accident has happen'd out;
> 'Tis not that I value the Money three Skips of a Louse;
> But the Thing I stand upon, is the Credit of the House;
> 'Tis true, seven Pound, four Shillings, and six Pence,
>   makes a great Hole in my Wages,
> Besides, as they say, Service is no Inheritance in these Ages.
> Now, Mrs *Dukes,* you know, and every Body understands,
> That tho' 'tis hard to judge, yet Money can't go without Hands.

Mrs Duke's response to this clumsy innuendo is a flood of tears! Here also the speaker's role is consistently and credibly sustained and it is only our perception of her limitations that prompts judgment of her.

The prologues of the Wife of Bath and the Pardoner in Chaucer's *Canterbury Tales* are so substantial that their place within

the overall narrative framework of the poem seems not to disqual-
ify them from treatment here. The Wife defends her five mar-
riages with a vigorous mixture of common sense, lusty joy in
sexuality and sophistical answering of authorities; then she tells
how she managed three of her five husbands with a stream of
abuse, accusations, arguments, flat contradictions, cajoling and
withholding of her favours in bed; and finally how her fifth husband, who was even better versed in authorities than herself,
played her with equal vigour at her own game until they reached
accord. Considered coolly, she is a monstrous egotist who will
have her way despite the happiness of her fellow-creatures or the
tenets of religion, but she is also full of vigorous life. By presenting
her through her own speech Chaucer allows us to experience
directly the impact of her personality; the torrent of words over-
whelms the reader as it did her unfortunate husbands.

We remarked that 'Fra Lippo Lippi' and 'My Last Duchess'
prompt sympathy and judgment in different proportions. In the
poems just described there is again a range: we heartily dislike
Lord All-Pride, think Mrs Harris a silly but amusing lady, and are
awestruck by the Wife of Bath. Many dramatic monologues
swing decisively to the pole of sympathy and aim primarily to
involve the reader in the sufferings of another. Browning wrote
such poems ('Evelyn Hope' and 'The Patriot') and so did Tennyson ('Tithonus' and 'Rizpah') but many critics, especially those
who base their definition on 'My Last Duchess', consider poems
where sympathy constitutes the main effect not to fall within the
category 'dramatic monologue', or to be imperfect instances of it.

Yet even in such poems the withdrawal of the poet seems to
encourage ironic reflection in the reader and we feel invited at
some point to adopt a judgment larger than the speaker's. This
may actually enhance the pathos of the speaker. 'The Affliction of
Margaret' by Wordsworth presents in fulsome and, to us, stilted
tones the lament of a mother who had not heard from her son for
seven years. The most alarming possibility that crosses her mind
is that he might prefer not to bother with her:

> Neglect me! no, I suffered long
> From that ill thought; and, being blind,
> Said, 'Pride shall help me in my wrong:
> Kind mother have I been, as kind
> As ever breathed': and that is true;
> I've wet my path with tears like dew,
> Weeping for him when no one knew.

But once in the poem this thought does not leave the reader, and Margaret's willingness to entertain various melodramatic alternatives helps to sustain it:

> Perhaps some dungeon hears thee groan,
> Maimed, mangled by inhuman men;
> Or thou upon a desert thrown
> Inheritest the lion's den.

Probably we also recall the analogous situation in Wordsworth's 'Michael'. Because we consider this possibility more boldly than Margaret we see beyond her, but o7r sympathy with her plight is increased by our awareness that she cannot face its worst aspect.

The irony takes another direction in 'The Chimney Sweeper' in Blake's *Songs of Innocence*. The speaker is a child sweep whose approach to his employment is a model of Christian acceptance:

> There's little Tom Dacre, who cried when his head,
> That curled like a lamb's back, was shaved: so I said
> 'Hush Tom! never mind it, for when your head's bare
> You know that the soot cannot spoil your white hair'.

Tom has a beautiful dream of angels and in the morning 'was happy and warm'. All this is entirely appealing as a child's innocent view of exploitation, but the reader's sympathy will make him the more likely to hold a strong opinion on such matters. Blake ensures such a response through the irony of the child's last line: 'So if all do their duty they need not fear harm.'

Such poems cannot usefully be divorced from other dramatic monologues. The artificiality of the attempt to draw a line here may be seen in Tennyson's 'Northern Farmer' poems. The 'New Style' farmer is very ironically presented. As his horse canters he hears 'Proputty, proputty, proputty' and his theme is an attempt to convince his son that he should marry for money rather than love. He contrives a religious justification: the poor steal and are lazy. His evidence for this is that his own father began with 'ammost nowt' but he admits, 'leästways 'is munny was 'id'. For this farmer money rather than effort is the source of wealth, and that is why he is prepared to disinherit his son if he marries against his wish. Yet, so far from softening or apologizing for such a doctrine, he expresses supreme satisfaction with the growth of his holdings and with his own materialistic marriage.

The 'Old Style' farmer, on the other hand, is affectionately portrayed. He likes his pint of ale, has indulged in the occasional sexual adventure and professes a somewhat limited notion of ethics - 'I done moy duty by Squoire an' I done moy duty boy hall' (sc. 'by all'). Nevertheless, he is an honest man who has lived life fully and worked hard to bring waste land into cultivation. Tennyson wants us to sympathize and to value the old-style yeoman virtues, whereas he sets an ironic distance between himself and the new-style farmer, but there is no essential difference in form.

A factor which has been implicit in our discussion so far but which is scanted by modern critics of dramatic monologue is that the speaker is very often used as a mouthpiece, more or less indirectly, for the poet's views. This is not an important aspect of 'My Last Duchess', though we may conclude from the poem that Browning prefers the qualities of the Duchess to those of the Duke. Lippo Lippi, though, is one of several speakers who talk about art in a way which, we know from elsewhere, had Browning's approval. When Lippi speaks of the physical world - 'The beauty and the wonder and the power,/The shapes of things, their colours, light and shades' - we sense that Browning is with him. Browning believed, like Lippi, that the soul of a man is comprehended best through his human individuality: that is his aim in his dramatic monologues. 'I always see the Garden and God there/A-making man's wife', Lippi says, and Browning held that the creative writer repeats in his proportion God's original act of creation when he sets forth men and women, not idealized but as they really are.

Sometimes the relationship between the speaker's and the poet's ideas is quite straightforward. Then dramatic monologue may be primarily a strategy by which a thought is given force by being proposed from the point of view of a speaker for whom it has special significance. Marvell adopts this approach in 'Bermudas', where his speakers are a group of puritans sailing to the Americas. Marvell's confidence in God's care for the true religion and delight in his wondrous gifts is expressed through the response of those who have good cause to appreciate them because of the striking beauty of their new-found home and the dangers they have passed. Hence too Yeats' poems spoken by Crazy Jane, a countrywoman whose unlettered simplicity enables her, like many literary fools, to challenge orthodoxy with basic wisdom about love, life and death. The dramatic persona has a more demotic voice and an earthier fund of experience than Yeats himself could credibly assume.

Sympathetic speakers in the vein of 'The Chimney Sweeper' and 'The Affliction of Margaret' are often designed, especially by the Romantic poets, to arouse concern for oppressed people. This is the purpose of Wordsworth's dramatic monologues in *Lyrical Ballads* - 'The Female Vagrant', 'The Last of the Flock', 'The Mad Mother'. Burns presented the deprivations of the Highlanders through their supposed words; Southey's 'Botany-Bay Eclogues' were regarded as revolutionary because their speakers blame the crimes for which they were transported upon society. These poems have lost most of their force because the causes they were advancing are now widely granted, but originally they were intended to engage the reader's sympathies in unaccustomed and unwanted directions and must have offered a considerable moral challenge.

At the other extreme from the sympathetic monologue is the satirical poem which promotes the poet's views by making the reader react against the speaker. Dramatic monologue is valuable here because the reader receives the impression that the speaker has full opportunity to state his case but is found wanting out of his own mouth, and because such speakers appear to be justifying themselves and hence sound smug and self-satisfied.

Extremity in religious matters seems specially to prompt the satirical monologue. In 'Johannes Agricola in Meditation' Browning exposes the presumption of the antinomian belief that God has chosen his elect and that they may therefore act as they please. Tennyson's 'St Simeon Stylites' is spoken by a fifth-century ascetic who seeks to guarantee sainthood by living on top of a pillar. His deprivations sound ridiculous and sordid and his pride and self-satisfaction show through. The hypocrisy in Burns' monologue 'Holy Willie's Prayer' is more blatant. The Scots Calvinist reflects cheerfully on how God 'Sends ane to heaven and ten to hell' and boasts of his zeal against drinkers, swearers, singing and dancing, but he expects God to overlook his own frequent sexual misdemeanours and to endorse his curses against his enemy in church politics.

In recent times the same target has been struck by the same method in Robert Lowell's poems 'After the Surprising Conversions' and 'Mr Edwards and the Spider'. Lowell exposes hell-fire theology by making its assumptions horrifyingly real in the sermon of a New England preacher:

As a small boy

On Windsor Marsh, I saw the spider die
When thrown into the bowels of fierce fire:
There's no long struggle, no desire
To get up on its feet and fly -
It stretches out its feet
And dies. This is the sinner's last retreat;
Yes, and no strength exerted on the heat
Then sinews the abolished will, when sick
And full of burning, it will whistle on a brick.

The stanza narrows down upon the destruction of the spider but then does not allow the dignity of a short line to the words 'And dies'. Instead the speaker hastens to link it with the 'abolition' of a human being and opens out the stanza again in vindictive triumph.

The most subtle means of representing the poet's opinions in dramatic monologue is by making them arise incidentally in the words of a speaker who only partially understands their significance. That is Browning's way in 'Fra Lippo Lippi' and in 'An Epistle containing the Strange Medical Experience of Karshish, the Arab Physician'. Karshish, who has met Lazarus after his return from death and is reporting back to the learned Abib, is hugely impressed by the story of Christ which he has been told but feels obliged to explain it in a way which takes account of Abib's scientific scepticism:

> 'Tis but a case of mania - subinduced
> By epilepsy, at the turning-point
> Of trance prolonged unduly some three days.

Towards the.end he asks 'Thy pardon for this long and tedious case' but finally he bursts out,

> The very God! think, Abib; dost thou think?
> So, the All-Great, were the All-Loving too -
> So, through the thunder comes a human voice
> Saying, 'O heart I made, a heart beats here!'

Karshish is made to seem direly in need of precisely the Christian revelation and its attractions are presented freshly with some of the excitement they must have held for its first adherents. Thus Browning suggests a corrective to contemporary attitudes, for Karshish's scientific scepticism parallels that which seemed to threaten religion in the nineteenth century. 'Journey of the Magi' by T.S. Eliot works similarly though it contrasts in tone. One of the Wise Men who visited Bethlehem realizes that something extraordinary occurred but has no way of knowing what:

> We returned to our places, these Kingdoms,
> But no longer at ease here, in the old dispensation,

With an alien people clutching their gods.
I should be glad of another death.

Again there is a contemporary parallel: the twentieth-century inquirer into Christianity may feel uneasy in the modern secular world and attracted by the idea of a new spiritual dimension but at a loss what to make of it all.

Tennyson's 'Lucretius' also makes an indirect approach to the poet's deepest concerns. The epicurean philosopher suffers a series of violently erotic visions which challenge his determined belief in his own rationality and afflict him with a brutal parody of his own materialism. Tennyson distrusted reason and was deeply opposed to materialism, but he did not believe that sensuality and despair - Lucretius commits suicide - are the necessary consequence. That is why he tells us at the start that Lucretius is reacting to a love-potion administered by his wife: such special circumstances inevitably qualify his attitudes in our eyes. Hence we are led to ponder upon those aspects of humanity which Lucretius ignores but Tennyson believes vital.

Such use of the monologue need not be regarded as merely a didactic device. It will not be necessary to observe that artistic creation is a strange and mysterious affair, and that a poet often comes upon his theme in its exact nuances only during the immediate struggle with the form he has chosen and the words which suggest themselves. The special requirements of dramatic monologue may prompt shades of meaning which might not otherwise have occurred to him. It enables him to gain a formal and emotional distance from his preoccupations.

Of course, it is impossible to see when the choice of dramatic monologue has added significantly to a poet's understanding of his own theme and, besides, we are running into untenable distinctions between form and content. However, in the course of this book the reader will remark a number of cases where poets have risen above their usual stature or extended their usual scope when writing in this genre. Consider Kipling, whose *Barrack-Room Ballads* are not generally taken seriously in studies of dramatic monologue. 'Loot' is addressed by an experienced soldier to a recruit and its initial appeal is in terms which the reader may well wish to repudiate:

> If you've ever stole a pheasant-egg be'ind the keeper's back,
>   If you've ever snigged the washin' from the line,
> If you've ever crammed a gander in your bloomin' 'aversack,
>   You will understand this little song o' mine.

The speaker is jovial to a fault but looting is not the most glorious aspect of imperial rule:

> When from 'ouse to 'ouse you're 'unting, you must always work in
>   pairs -
>   It 'alves the gain, but safer you will find -
> For a single man gets bottled on them twisty-wisty stairs,
>   An' a woman comes and clobs 'im from be'ind.'

It even transpires that the spoils are usually seized by the sergeant or quartermaster. Kipling's original readers probably favoured colonization as a way of spreading civilization and this poem should have perplexed them. There cannot be empires without armies and the speaker only behaves as armies usually do: he sees looting as "Ow to pay yourself for fightin' overtime'. If the reader wants an empire he must accept responsibility for the actions of his agents who, after all, are doing the dirty work.

Thus far in this chapter I have tried to open out a conception of dramatic monologue derived from certain of Browning's poems by remarking similar poems from before the Victorian period, the variety of possible proportions of sympathy and judgment and the use of the form as an oblique way of expressing the poet's ideas. The principal remaining aspect is disparities in the degree to which the speaker is dramatically realized: the concreteness of time and place, the presence or absence of an auditor, the colloquialness of the language, the amount of conflict or action. I have taken little account of this in the examples discussed in this chapter.

In my view it is difficult to talk about these factors with any precision and, with the methodology we have used so far, to perceive their significance. However, a couple of points may be made here. One is that the argument which associates the rise of dramatic monologue in the Victorian period with the drama is not, by itself, convincing. It is not clear that the condition of the theatre altered relevantly at that time and, anyway, there are many earlier dramatic monologues. Also, whilst it is true that Browning's monologues followed his relative failure in the theatre, many of Tennyson's appeared between 1875 and 1885 - during the period when his plays were being performed with some success.

Second, to define 'the dramatic' as 'like "Fra Lippo Lippi"' presumes a particular and limited notion of drama - Ibsenite naturalism. In such plays the characters speak and behave in a way which pretends to replicate, moment by moment, the things people literally say and do in actual physical and social life. This is a worthwhile dramatic tradition and it is notable that Browning, in so far as his poems suggest what might be done in a theatre, substantially anticipates it. But there are other ways of thinking about reality and other dramatic modes - those, say, of classical tragedy or modern Absurdist plays - which eschew the detail of daily life, reduce physical action to a minimum and allow the most fulsome heightening of language.

This thought helps us to appreciate the style of many dramatic monologues. Tennyson's most important uses of the form ('Ulysses' and 'Tithonus'; if we admit a brief narrative introduction, 'Oenone' and 'The Lotos-Eaters') are close in manner to lyric poems in his own person, and the situation of the speaker (though precise enough) draws upon fable and myth rather than social reality. In 'Tithonus' the speaker is the man who married the Dawn and was granted eternal life but forgot to ask for eternal youth - the story is from Ovid's *Metamorphoses*. The situation is the eastern sky and the occasion is each and every day - the repetition implied by diurnal sunrise adds to our sense of Tithonus' plight. His words are evocative and full with the imagery of the Dawn; his weariness and impotence are rendered more poignant by the sensuous location:

> I wither slowly in thine arms,
> Here at the quiet limit of the world,
> A white-hair'd shadow roaming like a dream
> The ever-silent spaces of the East,
> Far-folded mists, and gleaming halls of morn.

The dramatic action in the poem is a powerfully described sunrise; the auditor is the Dawn and her lack of response suggests her tragic inability to release Tithonus from his eternal doom:

> Lo! ever thus thou growest beautiful
> In silence, then before thine answer given
> Departest, and thy tears are on my cheek.

'Tithonus' has the literary manner of lyric poetry but then so, often, do *Oedipus at Colonus* and *Waiting for Godot*. This is the mode of Eliot's 'A Song for Simeon', Pound's 'La Fraisne' and very many earlier dramatic monologues. The individuality of the speaker is realized less concretely in naturalistic terms, but frankly poetic language may suggest more fully his emotional state. Such poems are varieties of dramatic monologue, not some other genre.

Tennyson's 'Locksley Hall' is not, like 'Tithonus', mainly a tone poem, but we will fail to appreciate it if we refuse to allow that dramatic speech may be rhetorical and lyrical as well as casual and colloquial. The opening is straightforward enough:

Comrades, leave me here a little, while as yet 'tis early morn:
Leave me here, and when you want me, sound upon the bugle-
                                                              horn.

We may imagine the repetition as the speaker's response to his friends' reluctance. But as he thinks back on his youth and Amy who lived in Locksley Hall he draws upon a wide stylistic range. Sometimes he is lyrical:

Love took up the glass of Time, and turn'd it in his glowing hands;
Every moment, lightly shaken, ran itself in golden sands.

When thinking of his youthful ideals he attempts noble rhetoric:

Till the war-drum throbb'd no longer, and the battle-flags were
                                                              furl'd
In the Parliament of man, the Federation of the world.

The 'poetic' quality of the language in 'Locksley Hall' tempts commentators to regard it as too thin a disguise for Tennyson to be true dramatic monologue, and they attribute to him the exaggerated stance of the poem. But there are clear hints that the speaker is to be regarded critically. His account is full of bitterness and rancour and he admits that some of his rhetoric is 'bluster'. He seeks to merge himself with the spirit of the age and eventually proclaims that 'the crescent promise of my spirit hath not set', but his 'long farewell to Locksley Hall' is linked with a curse and we doubt whether he has entirely come to terms with his past.

To expect dramatic monologue to limit itself to colloquial language is to impose a restriction which few literary forms have accepted, least of all drama. It is one of the several respects in which, as I have tried to show, a tight definition of the form creates artificial boundaries.

It will be perceived that my aim is to force the reader back upon the broad definition of dramatic monologue proposed at the start of this chapter. I believe that taking it as a poem in the first person spoken by someone who is indicated not to be the poet avoids separating 'My Last Duchess' from poems with which it has significant features in common and gives the best insight into the essential nature of the form.

This definition has the further advantage that the word 'dramatic' is utilised in a basic and clear-cut way, as distinguishing speech which is manifestly set up as a fiction from that spoken actually between people. The funeral orations by Brutus and Antony in *Julius Caesar* may be said to have certain 'dramatic' qualities - perhaps Antony's is 'more dramatic' in the senses that it makes a histrionic appeal to Caesar's wounds and blood, has sharp changes in pace and tone, uses suspense over the will, includes interaction with the people and physical movement when

Antony goes down among them, changes the direction of the play. Brutus' speech is relatively even and methodical. But both are utterly different from any real-life oration, however exciting the delivery or circumstances, and I am using 'dramatic' to express this basic distinction. Antony, though a fully conceived character, can never be human in the manner of an actual orator, Shakespeare, me the writer or you the reader, and this is fundamental in the way we perceive him. A similar difference exists between a monologue presented by Browning in his own person ('dramatic' though it may be in other senses, like 'One Word More') and a poem supposed to be spoken by Fra Lippo Lippi.

However, I recognize that some critics would make it a crucial test of a dramatic monologue that it should be dramatic in the way that Antony's oration, as opposed to Brutus', is. They may prefer a term such as 'lyrical monologue' or 'dramatic lyric' for poems like 'The Affliction of Margaret' and 'Mr Edwards and the Spider' - maybe for 'Tithonus' and 'Bermudas', since their problem is deciding where to draw a line - where the supposed speaker is not very strongly realized in a time and place with an auditor and an action. Such readers may maintain this distinction in their minds (though I hope to convert them) without affecting most of the argument. Others will find that I often remark that a speaker is given a weaker or stronger naturalistic presentation and should bear in mind that this is sometimes taken to be a crucial aspect.

3
Manners of speaking

In the previous chapter we explored the variety of uses of dramatic monologue starting from the liberal definition that it is a poem in the first person spoken by, or almost entirely by, someone who is indicated not to be the poet. We may now attempt to identify its essential qualities by comparing it with forms which are in some ways similar.

The crucial distinction is from the first-person lyric. A poem like Keats' 'Ode to a Nightingale' is located in time and space and quite dramatic; the difference is that there is nothing to suggest that it is not spoken by the poet, and when there is no such indication readers assume that the poet is the speaker. Of course, this does not mean that the poem is therefore subjective or autobiographical - the poet has complete freedom in the way he chooses to present 'himself'. We are not talking about the relationship between the poem and the poet's mind, but about the signals on the page to the reader about how he is to take the poem. Nor does it mean that we have to give entire credence to everything that is said - the poet may adopt a problematic stance initially and replace it eventually by another. Nevertheless, there is a particular quality in the mode of existence of the 'I' figure in such poems: he presents himself on the same plane of reality as the reader. He speaks to us or to himself with the same kind of directness that a man in the same room might do; or, rather, since he is inevitably on paper, in the way that a letter might do. He uses various literary manners and conventions, but there are conventions in speech and letter-writing too; the point is that the first person always constitutes a claim for the actual historical existence of the speaker.

The matter will become clearer if we compare the main alternative to the first-person lyric - third-person narrative. We may imagine a poem called 'How a Poet Heard the Nightingale'; it might begin, 'There was once a poet who was walking in Highgate Woods'. Such a poem seeks to establish a fictional world in which its characters live. This is not to say that the story may not describe actual events or quote people's actual words; the issue is the relationship between the reader and those events and words. Because they are within the framework of a narrative they are perceived as constituting another world. The characters do not speak to me, as it were, in my room, but to each other in other rooms which are like mine but sealed within the fictional world. When Keats says 'I cannot see what flowers are at my feet' we have the illusion at least of direct access to the experiencing poet. When we are told in a third-person narrative, 'It was so dark that Keats couldn't even distinguish the flowers around his feet', we must at once posit two levels of person: 'Keats' and the writer who has arranged the story. Characters and events are set apart from the reader by the structural suppositions of narrative. The posited writer is on our plane of reality and mediates between us and the action. 'Keats' becomes part of an alternative, created reality, a realm of fiction.

Dramatic monologue lurks provocatively between these two forms. The title, perhaps, and other hints as we go along indicate that the speaker is not the poet and hence has something to do with fiction; but the first-person mode makes an opposing claim for the real-life existence of the speaker on the reader's plane of actuality. There could be a dramatic monologue identical to 'Ode to a Nightingale' and just the title - 'The Romantic Poet Expatiates upon Hearing the Nightingale' - might be sufficient to make us read it with a mixture of sympathy and ironic judgment and seek to infer indirectly the poet's theme as we do in dramatic monologue. Here, I think, is the essential feature of the form.

Philip Sidney's famous answer to the accusation that the poet lies because he makes up stories is that 'he nothing affirms, and therefore never lieth'. The manifest fiction of the third-person narrative does not, other than in a temporary and trivial way, claim actuality. Rather, it offers an alternative world which relates to the actual world on a more sophisticated level of truth; it offers images of reality. But dramatic monologue does lie, for it sets up a fictional speaker whilst claiming for him, by the use of the first person, real-life existence. Käte Hamburger, to whose work on narrative strategies this analysis owes more than a little, uses the term 'feigning' (*The Logic of Literature,* pp. 55-9, 311-41). Dramatic monologue feigns because it pretends to be something other than what it is: an invented speaker masquerades in the first person which customarily signifies the poet's voice.

The concept of the feint, as distinct from the poet's 'I' figure on the one side and fiction on the other, enables us to see the significance of several features of dramatic monologue. It gives us a precise structure within which to contain the fact that the speaker is a convenient vehicle for the poet's opinions. We experience the 'I' of the poem as a character in his own right but at the same time sense the author's voice through him. The consequence of the frequent choice of an actual historical figure - Fra Lippo Lippi, for instance - also becomes apparent, for such a speaker has a mode of reality comparable with the poet's but nevertheless teasingly at odds with it.

The varying degrees of dramatic realization we have observed have the effect of moving the feint either towards the poet's 'I' or towards fiction. If there is a heavy apparatus of circumstantial detail which establishes for the speaker a world which we know is not the poet's, then the feint begins to approximate to fiction. If, alternatively, the speaker is relatively unlocated in time and place so that there is little beyond the title, say, to remind us that it is not supposed to be the poet speaking, then the feint is closer to the poet's 'I'.

It is fascinating to remark - and it makes clear the defining importance of the speaker who is indicated not to be the poet - that accumulation of dramatic detail has the opposite effect when the poem is spoken simply by the poet's 'I' figure. In 'Ode to a Nightingale' the concreteness of the situation and the poet's experience tends not to move Keats towards fiction, as in dramatic monologue, but to insist upon his status as a real-life person.

The presence of a silent auditor works similarly. In Wordsworth's 'Lines composed above Tintern Abbey' the fact that his sister is there with him makes Wordsworth more real to us. In dramatic monologue, however, the silent auditor tends to tilt the feint towards fiction because it provides more evidence that the speaker lives in a world of his own. But notice how direct dialogue shifts the mode decisively into fiction:

Wordsworth: In thy voice I catch
    The language of my former heart, and read
    My former pleasures in the shooting lights
    Of thy wild eyes.
Dorothy: Oh! William, behold
    In me what thou wast once, my dear, dear Brother!

Here, almost as much as in third-person narration, we are obliged at once to posit the framing figure of the author, for two speakers of equal status imply a third party who presents them and this sets them apart in a fictional world. The silent auditor is the most artificial and peculiar feature of dramatic monologue - that is why writers often prefer the more naturalistic letter form. We can now understand its rationale: it is useful to have another person present because he acts as a catalyst, obliging the speaker to respond to an immediate challenge, but the poem must not develop into dialogue because that would destroy the feint.

The significance of the narrative introduction which precedes some poems that are otherwise first-person monologues is also clear within this scheme. Properly, any narrative framework breaks the feint; in practice, though, if the ensuing monologue is sufficiently powerfully sustained, the feint reasserts itself. That is why I have allowed that such poems might fall within the general ambit of the genre.

Dramatic monologue may manifest a range of kinds of feint and the 'I' may be close to the poet or distanced by a wealth of fictional devices, but I do not think it is necessary to value one kind of balance above another on principle. We may, however, explore further its teasing and paradoxical nature.

There are various lengths to which the poet may go to establish his speaker. The title may do it, as in 'The Mower against Gardens' and 'The Bishop Orders his Tomb at St Praxed's Church' by Marvell and Browning. Often the speaker is distant in time and culture. 'The Bishop Orders his Tomb', Tennyson's 'Rizpah', Hardy's 'A Trampwoman's Tragedy' and Pound's 'Cino' and 'Scriptor Ignotus' actually have a date in the past as subtitle. The speaker may just have characteristics which we know are not those of the poet - many dramatic monologues are written by men from their idea of what is the feminine point of view.

The poet may provide for the speaker a language which is recognizably personal to him. The demotic exclamations of Lippi ('Boh!', 'Ouf!', 'Zooks!') are famous though perhaps not altogether successful. Kipling, Burns and Tennyson wrote monologues in dialect. Browning's Caliban in 'Caliban upon Setebos' is given a language which reflects his semi-human status - in particular, he usually speaks in the third person ('Conceiveth all things will continue thus'), presumably because he has not developed a full sense of his own identity. Skelton's 'Philip Sparrow' is spoken by a girl lamenting the death of her pet bird. The poem is a burlesque, mildly indecent and highly irreverent in its use of a mock-requiem, but the pretence of an innocent girl is sustained and her language is adduced as evidence of her good faith:

> For, as I tofore have said,
> I am but a young maid,
> And cannot in effect
> My style as yet direct
> With English words elect.

Sometimes the speaker has his own special imagery. In 'The Mower's Song' Marvell's speaker naturally talks about his mind in terms of his occupation:

> My Mind was once the true survey
> Of all these Medows fresh and gay;

> And in the greenness of the Grass
> Did see its Hopes as in a Glass;
> When *Juliana* came, and She
> What I do to the Grass, does to my Thoughts and Me.

The woman in D.H. Lawrence's 'Love on the Farm' speaks of sexual contact in a way which links her to the animal the man has trapped:

> With his hand he turns my face to him
> And caresses me with his fingers that still smell grim
> Of the rabbit's fur! God, I am caught in a snare!
> I know no what fine wire is round my throat.

In Tennyson's 'Tithonus' the fact that the lover is the Dawn gives rise to entirely germane and original sexual imagery:

> Thy cheek begins to redden thro' the gloom,
> Thy sweet eyes brighten slowly close to mine,
> Ere yet they blind the stars, and the wild team
> Which love thee, yearning for thy yoke, arise,
> And shake the darkness from their loosen'd manes,
> And beat the twilight into flakes of fire.

Browning's favourite device is to write so uncompromisingly from the speaker's perspective that it is hard for the reader to perceive what is happening. 'Andrea del Sarto' is spoken by a Renaissance painter to his wife. He is conscious of the deficiencies of his art (it is 'faultless' but lacking imaginative scope) and his attempts to please Lucrezia, his beautiful but unfaithful wife, lead him into compromise and dishonesty. The illusion that Andrea is the speaker is supported by his casual references to his life and contemporary figures and his sensitivity to his wife's reactions:

> And indeed the arm is wrong.
> I hardly dare - yet, only you to see,
> Give the chalk here - quick, thus the line should go!
> Ay, but the soul! he's Rafael! rub it out!
> Still, all I care for, if he spoke the truth,

(What he? why, who but Michael Angelo?
Do you forget already words like those?)
If really there was such a chance, so lost,
Is, whether you're - not grateful - but more pleased.
Well, let me think so. And you smile indeed!

The reader here must understand Andrea's attempt to alter Raphael's picture, his awareness that correcting the 'fault' may destroy the soul of the painting, the interruption of Lucrezia who doesn't remember the compliment paid by Michael Angelo, Andrea's fear that he may have lost the chance of becoming a great painter, his attempt to use this to gain a positive response from Lucrezia, and his probable self-deception in deciding to believe that her smile is indeed such a response.

It is not surprising that Browning's first readers accused him of obscurity; *The Spectator's* critic complained about 'his fashion of presenting incidents so allusively as to baffle ordinary penetration to discover what he means - of printing poems having reference to some facts or conversation not given and needed to explain them' (*Browning, The Critical Heritage,* p. 164). However, this strategy for forcing the reader to work his way fully into the speaker's point of view also affords the patient reader the imaginative pleasure of discovering the links between words and thoughts. Every poem is to an extent an exploration by the reader, who is invited to appreciate the interrelations of thought, image, rhythm and so on; dramatic monologue adds a further dimension, the task of following the thought of a speaker who is quite unaware of the reader.

It may seem that all this attention to the language and situation of the speaker establishes his existence as a fictional character, and it does tend that way. Yet at the same time, because the poem is in the first person and the speaker, we feel, should be the poet, a strong sense of the speaker's individuality is accompanied by a strong sense of the poem as feint. The more personal, expressive and relevant the remarks of the speaker, the more we are conscious of the artificiality of his making them. This awareness in the reader is supported by the manifest hints of egotism, bias and self-deception which, as we have seen, the poet often plants to make us see the speaker differently from the way he sees himself, and by the stylization of the poetic medium. Even the most colloquial monologues are plainly poems; the couplets in 'My Last Duchess' are unobtrusive but nevertheless there. We feel continuously the pressure of the poet's controlling mind.

This line of thought leads us to question a longstanding critical axiom about dramatic monologue: that the reader believes, or pretends to believe, that it is Fra Lippo Lippi or the Duke of Ferrara who speaks. Even critics who give due weight to the gap between the speaker's perception and the poet's nevertheless posit at some stage a belief in the actuality of the speaker. In my view this proposes an impossible reading experience: that we should be aware that the speaker is being placed by an agent outside the fictional world (not by other characters within it, which causes no problem), and at the same time credit him with attitudes independent of that agent. In fact a complex dramatic monologue like 'My Last Duchess' is experienced throughout by the sophisticated reader as a set-up. The speaker's words - the last lines about the statue of Neptune and the sea-horse, for instance - are understood as chosen strategically by the poet to promote aspects of his theme and feelings of attraction and withdrawal in line with the poet's preconceived ideas.

Let us take another example, 'The Bishop Orders his Tomb'. Here Browning's speaker is again a Renaissance figure: gravely ill, he is trying to ensure that his 'nephews' (illegitimate sons) give him the glorious monument he wants. In particular, he wishes to outdo a former rival - 'Old Gandolf with his paltry onion-stone, / Put me where I may look at him!' As well as nephews, the Bishop has acquired wealth, some of which he seems to have misappropriated from his church. This unChristian behaviour is pointed up by interspersed Biblical texts as his mind wanders:

> For Gandolf shall not choose but see and burst!
> Swift as a weaver's shuttle fleet our years:
> Man goeth to the grave, and where is he?
> Did I say basalt for my slab, sons?

Even more striking but altogether consistent is his unselfconscious Renaissance mixture of paganism and religion: on the frieze of his tomb he wants

> The Saviour at his sermon on the mount,
> St Praxed in a glory, and one Pan
> Ready to twitch the Nymph's last garment off,
> And Moses with the tables.

To some extent I feel with the Bishop in his extremity; I even have a flicker of disapproval at a churchman speaking thus (this might have been more important when the poem was written). These are the sympathy and judgment described in earlier chapters. But the Bishop is also a precisely posed figure of the Renaissance prelate, and my main response is amusement and admiration for Browning's economical contrivance. I don't believe that the Bishop would make quite such stark juxtapositions, but I recognize with excitement that they epitomize a whole attitude. Ruskin declared that the poem has 'nearly all that I said of the central Renaissance in thirty pages of the "Stones of Venice" put into as many lines' (*Browning, The Critical Heritage,* p. 198).

The over-determined element in dramatic monologue was recognized by early reviewers. One, defining 'Mr Browning's genius', termed him 'semi-dramatic':

> never quite dramatic, for we never lose sight of the critical eye of the poet himself, who discriminates all these different shades of thought, and tosses them off with a sharpness of outline, and sometimes an intellectual touch of caricature, often a sharp sarcasm, that could not have proceeded from the *inside* of the situation he is painting for us.

> (*Browning, The Critical Heritage,* pp. 288-9)

This awareness of the controlling poet is both general and, at moments, highly particular. The slightest touch can bring him suddenly into full focus - the last line about duty in 'The Chimney Sweeper'; the new-style Northern Farmer's admission that his father had hidden money; Lord All-Pride's claim for the 'Bliss' of sexual experience with him; Karshish's innocent observation that Lazarus 'affects the very brutes/And birds - how say I? flowers of the field'; the description by Eliot's Wise Man of 'three trees on the low sky'.

At such moments the poet obtrudes and the illusion of the feint is specially transparent. In 'The Bishop Orders His Tomb' it occurs particularly when the Bishop is made to speak of the Eucharist in a sensual but doctrinally correct way which is bound to startle anyone brought up in a protestant culture: 'And hear the blessed mutter of the mass,/And see God made and eaten all day long'.

Yet again, and I am trying to keep a balance, the Bishop is sufficiently there to call forth a warmth of human fellow-feeling. Indeed, Browning manages to make us feel closest to the Bishop at a point which, theoretically, does him little credit. His former mistress, the mother of his sons, is the most intimate and accessible factor in his life, revealing an ordinary human emotion which reaches across the cultural differences which Browning is so concerned to point up. It is still linked to his rivalry with Gandolf, but even this seems endearing in the last lines:

> And leave me in my church, the church for peace,
> That I may watch at leisure if he leers -
> Old Gandolf, at me, from his onion-stone,
> As still he envied me, so fair she was!

What we experience in dramatic monologue - and it is a quality which is not easily gained in other modes - is a divided consciousness. We are impressed, with the full strength of first-person presentation, by the speaker and feel drawn into his point of view, but at the same time are aware that he is a dramatic creation and that there are other possible, even preferable, perspectives. This condition is a precise consequence of the status of dramatic monologue as feint: we are obliged to posit simultaneously the speaking 'I' and the poet's 'I'.

This division of attention correlates in some poems with the balance between sympathy and judgment discussed earlier, and often it is promoted by our awareness that the speaker is being used partly to communicate the poet's views. But it is a characteristic of the feint and occurs even when the speaker is broadly sympathetic and presented mainly as an interesting character. Tennyson's Oenone (in the poem of that name) tells how Paris, her lover, was asked to choose who was the most beautiful goddess, and laments her loss now that he has left to pursue the promise of Venus that he should have Helen, the most beautiful woman in the world. However, Oenone cannot understand Cassandra's prophetic vision of armed men and a dancing fire which we take at once to be the fighting around Troy and its eventual destruction. We feel with Oenone in her distress but are separated from her by our larger knowledge.

Our approval may itself cause us to estimate a character otherwise than he does himself. Fra Lippo Lippi is almost diffident about his preference for naturalistic painting but we regard him as an important innovator. The church organist in Browning's 'Master Hugues of Saxe-Gotha', who is struggling to make sense of a baroque fugue as an image of life and is about to reach a significant truth when his candle goes out, asks 'Do I carry the moon in my pocket?' Of course not, but his meditations have been of no common order and he is able to afford much more illumination than he appreciates in his concern with how he will find his way down the stairs. Even when we agree with a speaker's estimate of himself there is likely to be a difference of timing. We probably anticipate in 'Locksley Hall' the speaker's confession, "tis well that I should bluster!' and in the Wife of Bath's Prologue her observation that Jesus 'spak to hem that wolde lyve parfitly;/And lordynges, by youre leve, that am nat I'.

There is an intrinsic poetic pleasure in the double perception stimulated by the feint in dramatic monologue. It is analogous to the ambiguous phrase or image in a lyric poem (though it may not be possible to track it down to a few syllables), and to the irony in a play or novel when a character is unaware of the full significance of his words in the light of the opinions or actions of others (though the monologue has little extension in time and only one speaker). It reflects the complexity of life, for it places the individual in a wider context of thought and events. On the one hand we have a powerful impression, through his own mind, of the kind of person the speaker is. On the other, we feel the pressure of an alternative way of viewing these matters and perhaps of an external force which threatens to qualify or even nullify the efforts of the speaker. The confidence of Browning's Duke and Bishop, Oenone, Swift's Mrs Harris - almost any speaker in a monologue - in the validity of their approach to the world and their own significance within it is challenged by our larger consciousness.

Such a reading experience is surely a salutary correction to the self-importance of almost everyone and if dwelt upon is likely to produce a teasing self-awareness. Indeed, one may begin to feel, in a simple regress, that oneself also could be under scrutiny. The reader of a dramatic monologue might well say with Vladimir in Becket's *Waiting for Godot*, 'At me too someone is looking, of me too someone is saying, He is sleeping, he knows nothing, let him sleep on'.

4

Super-monologues

From what has been said so far it might be inferred, correctly, that concentration of complex effects within a relatively small compass is a special quality of dramatic monologue. However, it may suffer from an associated limitation: it seems to work best in the fairly brief vignette, and this may debar it from the grander literary themes and keep it as an ultimately minor form. I think this is broadly true, but several poets have sought to expand its scope.

One may, of course, just write very long monologues. Browning did this in his later years but, partly for reasons of style and theme but also because of a lack of intensity, they are read only by specialists. Tennyson dealt with the issue in *Maud* (1855) by the same means that he used when writing in his own person in *In Memoriam*; he built up a poem from a series of short pieces spoken by his character over a period of time.

Each section of *Maud* establishes its own manner, drawing upon an individual selection of metres, line-lengths and stanzaic forms; each encapsulates a mood of the speaker as he reacts to changing circumstances. Since he is more than a little unstable the variety is extraordinary. He begins in brooding and morbid vein:

> I hate the dreadful hollow behind the little wood,
> Its lips in the field above are dabbled with blood-red heath,
> The red-ribb'd ledges drip with a silent horror of blood,
> And Echo there, whatever is ask'd her, answers 'Death'.

The apparent pureness of Maud leads him to criticize such self-indulgence in a more reflective tone:

> Yet, if she were not a cheat,
> If Maud were all that she seem'd,
> And her smile had all that I dream'd,
> Then the world were not so bitter,
> But a smile could make it sweet. (I.VI.x)

Her response moves him to wild lyrical excess:

> Rosy is the West,
>   Rosy is the South,
> Roses are her cheeks,
>   And a rose her mouth. (I.XVII)

Sometimes we see the speaker's attitude develop during a section, but often Tennyson plunges us deeply into his latest mood. The story is not easy to follow because we have to depend upon the speaker's strange perceptions: we are obliged to perform repeatedly the exercise of sympathetic attention by which the reader of dramatic monologue discovers the events to which the speaker is responding. This builds up into a weird reading experience, for we become aware that the speaker is unreliable - for instance, he abuses Maud's brother repeatedly, but eventually she is reported as saying he is 'rough but kind' (I.XIX.vii). He sees the world as composed only of perfect and wicked people and his perception even of objects varies alarmingly with his mood: within I.IV we read, 'A million emeralds break from the ruby-budded lime/ In the little grove where I sit'; and then, 'the whole little wood where I sit is a world of plunder and prey'; and then, 'Be mine a philosopher's life in the quiet woodland ways'. Sometimes his language switches from the mundane to the exotic within two lines:

> Your father is ever in London, you wander about at your will;
> You have but fed on the roses and lain in the lilies of life. (I.IV.x)

The leaps from section to section and in the speaker's mind weaken our sense of an objective world of people and events; the real action is inside his head. At the same time, his obsessive repetition of imagery of flowers, animals and stones, often in exotic words and provocative metaphors, encourages us to discover continuity and coherence in recurring images. They form associative connections at an imaginative level independent of the rational, sequential syntax of everyday language so that we enter into a play of impressionistic tones as intuitive and kaleidoscopic as the speaker's mind. The capacity of dramatic monologue to draw the reader into an alien pattern of thought is nowhere more fully exploited.

The principal alternative means of developing dramatic monologue is by combining into a greater whole monologues by different characters. Arthur Hugh Clough's *Amours de Voyage* (published 1858) is made up of letters written by people travelling in Italy - Claude and Mary, who meet and are attracted to each other, and Mary's sister. The poem stretches the concept of dramatic monologue, but is admissible since the characters never write to each other but to silent third parties. In fact, Claude and Mary conspicuously fail to achieve any real contact: in the early part of the poem they are at cross-purposes and later on they fail to meet again despite diligent inquiries and the sending and leaving of messages.

The tone of *Amours de Voyage* could hardly be less like *Maud*, for Claude is intellectual, troubled, unsure of himself, wary of commitment and perhaps sexuality. His letters are self-analytical to the point where action is crippled; Mary and her sister mingle traveller's chat with maidenly caution, overflowing into enthusiastic but coy postscripts. Above all, nothing happens - at least to the principals: Rome, contrastingly, suffers revolution and invasion. Yet Claude is aware of his limitations and finally there seems to be a perverse integrity in his refusal of commitment in such a shifting world:

I will look straight out, see things, not try to evade them;
Fact shall be fact for me, and the Truth the Truth as ever,
Flexible, changeable, vague, and multiform, and doubtful. (V.v)

This is partly because religion, Claude's other preoccupation, is equally unreliable, but also because the blocked dramatic mode

of the poem - letters which are unread by the person they most concern - establishes for the reader a universe of half-opportunities
and ruined aspirations (the Romans' as well as Claude's). Towards the end he tries to throw off 'this sad, self-defeating depen-
dence' and wonders, 'After all, perhaps there was something
factitious about it' (V.viii). The reader is left to decide whether
this is maturity or despair.

Clough adds a further perspective in *Amours de Voyage*: it is
arranged in five cantos each introduced and closed by a short
poem in heightened lyrical style ('Therefore farewell, ye hills, and
ye, ye envineyarded ruins!'). This traditional literary language,
implying the more generous vistas of emotion usually celebrated
by poets, is set against the cautious lives of the characters. But
who is the writer of these passages? Their structural role suggests
it is the poet and this seems to threaten the feint, but the envoy at
the end ('Go, little book!') links him with a teasing uncertainty
about the mode of reality of the whole poem: the external voice
which seems to place Claude finally threatens to merge with him.

In *The Ring and the Book* (1868-9) Browning combines ten
long monologues by nine speakers all concerned with the same set
of events. Here again, the effect of developing dramatic monologue is to throw emphasis onto its tendency to raise questions
about the status of the speaker and the nature of perception. The
speakers are all concerned with a trial - an attempt to discover and
judge what happened - but almost all their accounts are partial.
Count Guido is accused of murdering his wife Pompilia and his
principal defence is provocation - that her supposed parents mis-
led him before the marriage about her wealth, and that she
deserted him and committed adultery with a young priest, Caponsacchi. The reply of Pompilia, given from her deathbed, and of
Caponsacchi is that Guido mistreated her and that the priest
merely rescued her. Each side has a lawyer; Pompilia's is particularly perverse, for he is unable to accept that she might be truthful
and, to gain opportunity to display his forensic skill, admits many
of the charges against her. There are three observers: 'Half-Rome'
supports Guido but eventually indicates prejudice in that he is

doubtful of the fidelity of his own wife; 'The Other Half-Rome' supports Pompilia but reveals that he has a grudge against Guido over a financial matter; 'Tertium Quid' pretends to be impartial but is mainly concerned to impress his influential listeners with the sophistication and elegant phraseology of his analysis.

It might seem that Browning's aim in giving each character his own monologue is to demonstrate the relativity of the perception of events and hence of moral judgments - that we are to regard each speaker as having a case when the matter is considered from his point of view. To an extent this is so and we may find ourselves in sympathy temporarily with most of the characters. Nevertheless, Browning makes it perfectly clear in a preliminary book written in his own person that Pompilia is entirely pure and innocent, and Guido eventually admits not only to the deed with which he is charged but to a selfish, immoral and atheistic attitude to life.

Browning's theme is human nature. He defines its limits by the innocence of Pompilia and the wickedness of Guido (both made more extreme than in the source material for the purpose), and sets between them the painful struggle towards truth of action and judgment by a few and the petty fallibility of the majority. By keeping the facts constant (and he stresses that they actually happened) Browning exhibits in their own words the influences which lead the observers and lawyers to prevaricate and compromise and Caponsacchi impulsively and idealistically to make a stand. The speaker closest to Browning's view is the aged Pope, to whom Guido appeals. He is deeply aware of human fallibility, his own included, and that "twixt the best and worst . . . crowd the indifferent product, all too poor/ Makeshift, starved examples of humanity!' (Penguin edition, 1974, X, 1212-14). But he declares,

> White shall not neutralise the black, nor good
> Compensate bad in man, absolve him so:
> Life's business being just the terrible choice. (X, 1235-37)

Nothing can absolve men from the duty to seek the truth.

By setting his characters against each other - and it is not possible to demonstrate here the intricate web of ironic cross-references in their monologues - Browning illustrates their fallibility and obliges us to conduct an analysis of the case like that undertaken by the Pope. He declares after reading the documents,

> Truth, nowhere, lies yet everywhere in these -
> Not absolutely in a portion, yet
> Evolvable from the whole: evolved at last
> Painfully, held tenaciously by me. (X, 228-31)

The truth we must painfully evolve from the poem is not simply that which would enable us to find Guido innocent or guilty - like the Pope, we see that almost at once. Browning would have us discover the relationship between human affairs and ultimate truth. This latter, for Browning and the Pope, exists in its full and absolute immensity in God; men can only piece together the fragments as they appear in this world (X, 1307-40). Nevertheless, it is our task to make what moral coherence we can of the world and the poem, holding fast to instances such as Pompilia. Browning believed that 'The moral sense grows but by exercise' (X, 1414) and intended us to benefit from reading *The Ring and the Book*.

Thinking of piecing together fragments affords a link to a last instance of the specially developed monologue. My tidy and purposeful account of *The Ring and the Book* belies its devious and introverted style and its great length. Eliot's *The Waste Land* (1922) is contrastingly spare and compressed but is also a sequence of dramatic monologues which challenges the reader to discern connections. We can distinguish clearly the speeches of Marie at the beginning, the barmaid in the second section and Tiresias in the third. For much of the remainder it is difficult to be sure who is speaking, or even when one speaker ceases and another begins. Vastly more than in *Maud*, the traditional continuities of character, time and place upon which a poem like 'Fra Lippo Lippi' is founded are displaced by a mode of organization based directly on images and themes. Moreover, the disrupted vision of *The Waste Land* is presented not as the reflection of a distorting mind (as in *Maud*) or as the raw material of life among which moral truths are to be discerned (as in *The Ring and the*

Book). This is how Eliot believes the world is: scarcely embodied voices competing for attention and speaking only of frustration and squalor.

The present chapter might easily be amplified in order to posit a sequential development related to general movements in literary sensibility. In the nineteenth century dramatic monologue assumes unprecedented importance but almost at once the feint is exploited self-consciously to express dissatisfaction with common-sense assumptions about the nature of consciousness and of the world. The historical development of dramatic monologue is the subject of the second part of this study.

5
Before the Victorians

Dramatic monologue was not recognized as such until the Victorians but its tradition was nevertheless long and firm. In Roman times and into the nineteenth century it was called 'prosopopoeia' and generally practised in schools, following Quintilian's recommendation (*Institutio Oratoria*, III, viii, 49-54). He thought it useful training for orators because one must bear in mind the rank, achievements and character of the individual represented. The most important literary forms of prosopopoeia were the complaint, the epistle and the humorous colloquial monologue.

It is at this point that the reader who believes that a high degree of naturalistic presentation is a defining quality of dramatic monologue will feel most concerned. It is true that the speaker in many of the poems discussed here is weakly realized; it is a principal part of my argument that there is an increasing use of naturalistic features. However, I see no essential difference of form and prefer to consider all first-person poems where the speaker is indicated not to be the poet as dramatic monologue. The unconvinced reader may, if he chooses, regard doubtful instances as 'precursors of dramatic monologue'. My main aim is to establish a historical continuity; terminology is not important.

The complaint was originally an expression of grief or disappointment about love or death or both. It may be traced back to Theocritus and other Greek pastoral poets of the third century BC; it was developed by Virgil in his *Eclogues*. The poet may complain in his own person or there may be a full dramatic distinction of poet and speaker, as in Theocritus' complaint of Polyphemus, the one-eyed Cyclops, about his unrequited love for a sea-nymph. Very often there is a light pretence that the speaker is a shepherd or some other figure in an idealized pastoral situation.

In the Renaissance the complaint flourished in its lyric, dramatic and pastoral modes. Almost all the major English poets wrote them; examples include Milton's 'Lycidas', Marvell's Mower poems, 'A Lover's Complaint' by Shakespeare and several poems by Spenser. The collection *England's Helicon* (1600) contains dozens of pieces where minor writers affect the stances of love-lorn nymphs and shepherds. The complaint by a historical figure was hugely popular in *The Mirror For Magistrates* (1559-1610), a compilation of stories of the downfall of kings and barons told in their own persons with sketchy introductions. Already in the fifteenth century we find complaints supposedly by the Duchess of Gloucester, Henry VI and Edward IV. John Lydgate made some use of the first person in *The Fall of Princes* (1438).

The Renaissance complaint usually requires of the reader some sympathetic involvement with the afflictions of another, but there may also, in accord with the prevailing theory of the function of poetry, be didactic implications about how such misfortunes may be avoided or in what spirit they should be faced. In Daniel's 'Complaint of Rosamond' he is told,

> Report the downe-fall of my slippry state:
> Of all my life reveale the simple truth,
> To teach to others, what I learnt too late:
> Exemplifie my frailtie, tell howe Fate
>   Keepes in eternall darke our fortunes hidden,
>   And ere they come, to know them tis forbidden.

In the eighteenth century sympathetic identification with the emotions of another came to be valued in itself as the foundation of moral sensibility. An influential theory was that man is motivated by feeling rather than reason and hence that consideration for others can derive only from a full imaginative appreciation of the consequences of one's actions for others. With this was associated a greater humanitarian concern for the weak and oppressed.

These attitudes stimulated an extension in the use of the dramatic complaint to arouse the reader's sympathetic involvement with a speaker. A series of deprived figures present their woes in the poems of Collins, Warton, Gray, Cowper, Burns, Blake, Wordsworth, Coleridge and Southey so that the reader may indulge his sentiments and attune his moral responses.

These monologuists cultivated the exotic as a way of evoking fresh emotions and as a justification for a more fulsome style. It may be regarded as an adaptation of the pastoral mode. In a preface to his *Persian Eclogues* (1742) Collins explained his use of Oriental poetry: 'There is an elegancy and wildness of thought which recommends all their compositions; and our geniuses are as much too cold for the entertainment of such sentiments as our climate is for their fruits and spices'. The second eclogue (notice how the term reflects Collins' awareness of the tradition of Theocritus and Virgul) is a dramatic monologue in which Hassan, a cameldriver, complains about his mental and physical sufferings as he crosses the desert; it was his desire for gold which made him leave pleasant vales and his betrothed. We are expected to benefit by sharing his sentiments - the Ciceronian motto to the first edition suggested that such reading should broaden the sympathies and enlighten the understanding.

Joseph Warton followed the same approach in 'The Dying Indian' (*c.*1747). This poem succeeds strikingly in portraying a mind from another culture, for the Indian is defiantly opposed to Christianity as he has seen it practised by colonial Spain: 'I ne'er have worshipp'd/With those that eat their God' (did Browning remember this when he wrote 'The Bishop Orders his Tomb'?). Cowper similarly seeks our sympathy with the exotic oppressed in 'The Negro's Complaint' (1788), the young Coleridge wrote 'The Complaint of Ninathóma' and Wordsworth included 'The Complaint of a Forsaken Indian Woman' in *Lyrical Ballads*. Many of the hugely popular poems of Mrs Felicia Hemans were in the vein of *Lays of Many Lands,* which she published in 1826.

These speakers are noticeably more specific in name, qualities and circumstances than the usual Renaissance complainant, presumably because the poet must convince us of the actuality of the character in order to secure a full emotional engagement. This may also account for an increasing emphasis on the detail of the dramatic situation. Collins' 'Hassan' is preceded by a note of the time and place and begins with a description of the desert. The dramatic realization of Gray's poem 'The Bard' (1757) was sufficient to give rise to a number of paintings of the scene, 'On a rock, whose haughty brow/Frowns o'er old Conway's foaming flood'. The narrative framework is intrusive and the speaker is particularized by his physical and historical situation rather than personally, but the poem shows the sentimental and exotic interests of the eighteenth century flowing into Romanticism and stimulating a more dramatic presentation of the speaker. The bard calls to Edward I who is passing at the head of his conquering army and foresees the vicissitudes of English history and the accession of the Tudor line. Finally he plunges to his death 'Deep in the roaring tide'. Gray even takes his dramatic pretence to the length of assuming a great deal of historical detail which was bound to baffle his readers; like Browning, he was accused of obscurity. This historical dimension reminds us of *The Mirror for Magistrates*. Thinking of the continuity of the form, we may also notice that Gray was very interested in Lydgate at the time when he wrote 'The Bard'. In an unpublished essay he quoted several passages from *The Fall of Princes* where a character is supposed to speak, admitting Lydgate's 'art in raising the more tender emotions of the mind'.

The dramatic monologue which seeks the reader's sympathetic involvement is taken to its full development by Southey at the end of the century in his *Monodramas*. All the speakers are on the point of suicide and they address fully identified auditors in specific circumstances about the immediate pressures which are causing them to take their lives. They are all from exotic climes but the emotions are varied quite credibly - Ximalpoca, a defeated Mexican king, is stoical, La Caba, the victim of rape and treachery, is desperate, the Wife of Fergus, who has killed her adulterous husband, is defiant. The style is relatively formal, though not more so than most of Tennyson's dramatic monologues. Southey attempts to imitate the associative connections and interruptions of the mind in movement. 'La Caba' begins:

> Father! Count Illan! here - what here I say, -
> Aloft ... look up! ... aye, father, here I stand,
> Safe of my purpose now! The way is barr'd; -
> Thou need'st not hasten hither!

This may seem crude, but it is plainly the link between Daniel's 'Complaint of Rosamond' and 'Locksley Hall'.

The dramatic epistle is born fully grown in Ovid's *Heroides*. This is a sequence of letters mostly supposed to have been written by love-lorn women - there are also three pairs of lovers - at crucial points in their histories. We have 'Penelope to Ulysses', 'Phaedra to Hippolytus', 'Oenone to Paris', 'Dido to Aeneas', 'Deianira to Hercules', 'Medea to Jason', 'Sappho to Phaon', and exchanges between Paris and Helen and Hero and Leander. The feint of the speaker is consistently maintained, her situation is specific and detailed, and she keeps the intended recipient clearly in mind. The subtlety and fulness of the portrayal is altogether similar to that of later monologuists, though the occasions and emotions are relatively limited.

Ovid's epistles were translated into English by George Turberville (1567) and Dryden (1680). Daniel and Donne wrote notable poems in the mode. Daniel's 'Letter from Octavia to Marcus Antonius' (1599) shrewdly presents Octavia as a rather ordinary woman who quite fails to understand the attractions of Cleopatra - 'What fault have I committed?' she asks. We think it unlikely that her arguments will have much effect. Donne (if it be he - the attribution is disputed) takes up Sappho but with typical boldness exploits her reputed homosexuality by giving her a letter to a woman. Witty play combines with sympathetic imagery and some subtle exploration of a narcissistic element in Sappho's feeling:

> Likenesse begets such strange selfe flatterie,
>   That touching my selfe, all seemes done to thee.

My selfe I embrace, and mine owne hands I kisse,
  And amorously thanke my selfe for this.
  Me, in my glasse, I call thee; But, alas,
When I would kisse, teares dimme mine *eyes*, and *glasse*.

The Ovidian epistle obviously overlaps with the dramatic complaint and may be regarded as a special instance of it. The first of Southey's *Monodramas* is spoken by Sappho, one of Ovid's heroines, and one of the passages in Lydgate's *Fall of Princes* which Gray praises is Canace's letter, which he compares with the version in the *Heroides*. However, Ovid did not attempt to suppress the light and witty strain in his style and his epistles more often than the complaint go beyond sympathy to exploit the divided awareness which is inherent in dramatic monologue. Often we appreciate that the perspective of the speaker is limited by factual ignorance or personal inadequacy.

When Phaedra writes in an attempt to seduce her stepson Hippolytus we are conscious continually of the remainder of the story - Hippolytus rejects her, she accuses him to Theseus, Theseus curses him and he is destroyed by a wild bull from the sea. Phaedra makes repeated references to bulls, for Europa and Pasiphae were among her forebears. We are also made to perceive her self-deception. She dwells upon the power and brutality of Theseus in order to justify her disloyalty, but it does not occur to her that his vengeance will be terrible. Her mythological illustrations are extremely ill-chosen, for they concern instances where sexual passion resulted in death through an animal or a member of the family (Cephalus, Adonis, Meleager). She thinks she is making an eloquent case but we are conscious of her self-deception and of the doom which will befall the family. Repeatedly in the *Heroides* personal emotion is set against external factors which are known to the reader but not to the speaker. We have almost a tragic sense of people caught up in situations that are beyond their knowledge and certainly their control.

One of the more substantial imitations of the *Heroides* is Michael Drayton's *England's Heroicall Epistles* (1619). Here a series of lovers from English history - mainly the Wars of the Roses -

exchange letters expressing their relationship and their attitudes to the circumstances which separate them. The work has affinities with *The Mirror for Magistrates* in style, unfortunately, as well as historical perspective, but sometimes Drayton hits upon a vivid character and manner of treatment. Because of his interest in history he makes his speakers allude to their affairs without any special consideration for the reader, who has to be assisted by endnotes; like 'The Bard', this anticipates Browning's method of drawing us into the speaker's mind. Above all, for our understanding of the development of dramatic monologue, Drayton imitates Ovid's play upon the gap between our knowledge and the attitude of the speaker.

Queen Isabel, wife of the deposed Richard II, writes to him from France. Whatever the rights of the matter it is agreed that he was less than competent, but she thinks him a paragon. She believes determinedly that, had Bolingbroke and Mowbray been allowed to fight, Bolingbroke would have been killed, though no one could be sure of such a result; she curses the day the tournament was forbidden without mentioning that it was Richard's weakness, personal and political, that caused this to happen. She declares that Bolingbroke's father was illegitimate, a story which Drayton says was circulated out of 'meere Spight and Malice'; and she treats simply as murder the deaths of Scroope, Greene and Bushy who, in the words of Drayton's note, were executed 'as vile persons, which had seduced the King to this lascivious and wicked life'. The Queen's bias is manifest but appealing because it demonstrates her continuing devotion to her fallen husband. Most of Drayton's epistles are less interesting than this, but he is equally acute and in quite another manner in the correspondence between Edward IV and Mistress Shore. The King, who has seen the notorious lady only once, professes love but manages to write most of the time about wealth. In reply she pretends fidelity to her husband but hardly disguises her eagerness. History performs the same function for Drayton as mythology for Ovid: it enables the poet to use the reader's prior knowledge to place the attitudes of the speaker.

Pope's 'Eloisa to Abelard' is the most important dramatic monologue in English before the nineteenth century and the most important successor to the *Heroides*. Commentators have been at pains to deny that it is dramatic monologue, but I believe it satisfies the most demanding criteria with the exception of the actual presence of an auditor. Even in this respect, Eloisa's sensitivity to the likely response of Abelard, her reader, makes his influence more real than the auditor in many monologues. Langbaum, who sees the gap between the perceptions of speaker and reader as the special quality of Victorian dramatic monologue, objects that Eloisa 'understands herself as an observer would understand her' and that at the end she is made to reach a '*right* conclusion' which is determined independently of her character (*The Poetry of Experience*, pp. 143, 150).

It is true that Eloisa understands the general nature of her conflict. Forced into a convent, she admits 'All is not Heaven's while Abelard has part,/Still rebel nature holds out half my heart'. However, her divided allegiance is sometimes more apparent than she thinks, and especially towards the end of the poem, though this is where Langbaum believes the '*right* conclusion' - the choice of religious duty - occurs. She imagines the voice of 'a sainted maid' calling her to join the dead:

> 'But all is calm in this eternal sleep;
> Here grief forgets to groan, and love to weep,
> Even superstition loses every fear:
> For God, not man, absolves our frailties here.'

This sounds Stoic rather than Christian: Eloisa's life after death is neither heavenly nor purgatorial but a thankful oblivion. And what is the 'superstition'? Presumably the attitude of the Church. Her submission to duty is equally uncertain in the passage which follows:

> I come, I come! prepare your roseate bowers,
> Celestial palms, and ever-blooming flowers.
> Thither, where sinners may have rest, I go,
> Where flames refined in breasts seraphic glow:

> Thou, Abelard! the last sad office pay,
> And smooth my passage to the realms of day;
> See my lips tremble, and my eyeballs roll,
> Suck my last breath, and catch my flying soul!

This is as erotic as any passage of the poem, more of a *liebestod* than a saintly renunciation of the fleshly life. She catches herself in her excess: 'Ah no - in sacred vestments mayst thou stand,/ The hallowed taper trembling in thy hand'; yet she allows a further hint of sexual awareness to escape her: 'It will be then no crime to gaze on me'. Finally she imagines visitors to their tomb - not pilgrims to celebrate her Christian submission but 'two wandering lovers', and envisages a poet who may tell their story - not a religious devotee but one 'who loves so long, so well'. Both Eloisa and Pope are ambivalent about the '*right* conclusion' and the uncertainty is communicated to the reader precisely because Eloisa does not understand quite everything. The mode of the *Heroides* proves very fruitful and deserves a full place in a study of dramatic monologue.

Some humorous colloquial monologues - our third group - have already been considered: the Wife of Bath's Prologue, 'Mrs Harris' Petitition', 'Holy Willie's Prayer', Tennyson's Northern Farmers. This line also begins with Theocritus. In his second idyll a woman is trying to cast a spell on Delphis, her chosen man:

> First barley glows on the fire. More, Thestylis,
> throw more on. Where are you, idiot? Head in the clouds?
> Am I to be laughed at by you as well, you wretch?
> Scatter them, and chant, 'These are Delphis' bones.'
>
> (*Greek Pastoral Poetry,* trans. Anthony Holden,
> Harmondsworth, 1974)

The poem is a down-beat reflection of Theocritus' love complaints; this kind of monologue very often implies the comic deficiency of the speaker in comparison with the loftier attitudes which are customary in the literary form. This is part of the point of Rochester's 'Very Heroical Epistle from my Lord All-Pride': we contrast All-Pride's attitude with those of Ovid's ladies. Burns seeks the same kind of effect in his 'Epistle from Esopus to Maria' (1794). Esopus is the actor James Williamson who had been imprisoned for vagrancy; he writes to Mrs Maria Riddell, once a friend of Burns but now an enemy. Esopus' words suggest his bombastic style of acting ('From these dire scenes my wretched lines I date') and his praise of Maria exposes her faults ('Who christen'd thus Maria's lyre divine/The idiot strum of vanity bemused?').

Tennyson and Browning are the heirs and in major ways the beneficiaries of these three traditions. The humorous colloquial monologue and the dramatic epistle as Browning uses them in 'Soliloquy of the Spanish Cloister' and 'Karshish' might have been invented independently, but the early work of both poets shows a clear connection with the complaint. Browning had written 'The First-Born of Egypt' by 1827: the poem is an account by one of the Hebrews of the final plague visited by Jehovah upon the Egyptians. It is exotic and melodramatic in the manner of Collins and Southey, as are several of the poems in Tennyson's adolescent *Poems by Two Brothers* (1827) – 'Antony to Cleopatra' (at the point of death), 'Mithridates presenting Berenice with the Cup of Poison', 'Lamentation of the Peruvians' and 'Written by an Exile of Bassorah, while sailing down the Euphrates'. Tennyson also has 'The Druid's Prophecies', where a bard of Anglesey foresees the fall of the Romans. It was out of a thorough acquaintance with the eighteenth-century and Romantic monologue of sentiment that the Victorians fashioned their first attempts.

Above all, Tennyson's 'Oenone' (1832) is derived directly and substantially from Ovid, who has a letter from her to Paris. There are great similarities of situation and phrasing and our larger knowledge of the story is exploited in the same kind of way, though Tennyson uses spoken lament rather than the epistle. He also moves away from the human realism of Ovid's character, who is not above malicious jibes against Helen, and creates his own tone, incantatory, evocative, ornate. So far from discovering a new form, Tennyson adapts an old one to his preferred emotional timbre. We should also notice 'Hero to Leander', published 1832.

Appreciation of pre-Victorian dramatic monologue continues beyond Tennyson. Swinburne derives 'The Complaint of Lisa' from Boccaccio and in 'Anactoria' returns to Sappho; like Donne, he has her addressing another woman. Matthew Arnold even has 'A Modern Sappho': she soliloquizes in a situation close to Ovid's but in a contemporary setting. Pound reminds us of Tennyson's 'Oenone' and of Ovid and Theocritus in his early poem, 'An Idyll for Glaucus'. Here a nymph laments the loss of her fisherman lover. We, who have access to the legend, know that he has become a sea-god and that she missed her chance to join him when she declined to eat the transforming grass he offered her: 'I wonder why he mocked me with the grass'.

Pound is a valuable figure on whom to end this survey because he admired Turberville's translation of the *Heroides* and, in a review of Eliot's 'Prufrock', recognized a continuous tradition: 'Antiquity gave us Ovid's *Heroides* and Theocritus's woman using magic. The form of Browning's *Men and Women* is more alive than the epistolary form of the *Heroides*. . . . Mr Eliot has made two notable additions to the list' (*Literary Essays,* London, 1954, pp. 227-9, 419-20).

6
The Victorians

Dramatic monologue had an unprecedented importance for the Victorians though, as I have shown, there is no single aspect of it which was not anticipated. Critics who see it as the special invention of Browning and Tennyson offer two competing explanations, each starting from the Romantic movement.

Robert Langbaum, in *The Poetry of Experience,* stresses the separation of poet and speaker and relates it to Romanticism, which he describes as a loss of absolute sanctions in spiritual, moral and social matters, forcing individuals to fall back upon subjective experience to establish values by which to live. The Victorian poet, he argues, has even less confidence in general truths than the Romantic, and in dramatic monologue explores, with a historical and psychological awareness, the different positions that have been held by various men. Thus dramatic monologue is 'an appropriate form for an empiricist and relativist age, an age which has come to consider value as an evolving thing dependent upon the changing individual and social requirements of the historical process' (pp. 102-3). J. Hillis Miller in *The Disappearance of God* (Harvard/Oxford, 1963) also refers to the loss of absolute values and sees dramatic monologue as a means of trying out a range of beliefs. He terms Browning's method 'historicism', the notion that one 'can approach an absolute vision only by attempting to relive, one by one, all the possible attitudes of the human spirit' (p. 107). This is not relativism, which confesses itself at a loss and views all judgments as tentative (Langbaum's position), but a positive and hopeful quest for the overriding perspective which may eventually achieve 'that opaque, ambiguous, multiple thing, reality'.

The objection to these arguments is that Tennyson and Browning often have a preferred opinion and use the monologue to promote it. This does not suggest that it has a special connection with bewilderment about values. Langbaum and Miller make much of their case from *The Ring and the Book*, but many readers feel that the poem is less a perplexed exploration of a neutral world than a purposive demonstration of *a priori* convictions (this is the view I took in chapter 4).

It is argued alternatively that the attention given to dramatic monologue in the Victorian period and the tendency to distinguish clearly speaker and poet represent a reaction against Romantic subjectivity, a wish to move out from the poet's own emotions into an objectively perceived world. R.E. Prothero, summarizing Browning's achievement in 1890, termed his poetry 'a counter-irritant to that poison of subjectivity which impels poets to shut themselves up in the maze of their own personal experiences, and to humanize Nature because they cannot dramatise Man' (*Browning, The Critical Heritage*, p. 521).

The case that Browning is a robust objective poet in reaction against the inward-looking tendency of Romanticism is put by Philip Drew in his book *The Poetry of Browning* (chs 1, 3). He leans especially upon the essay Browning wrote in 1852 to introduce an edition of letters supposed to be Shelley's. There Browning distinguishes the subjective and the objective poet. The latter seeks 'to reproduce things external (whether the phenomena of the scenic universe, or the manifested action of the human heart and brain) with an immediate reference, in every case, to the common eye and apprehension of his fellow men'. Such poetry 'in its pure form' is called 'dramatic' and Shakespeare is a supreme instance. Drew believes that Browning meant to be this kind of poet, one who draws upon the world around him as he observes it rather than upon an inner vision.

This theory leaves an awkward sense that the individuality of the speakers should somehow be connected positively with Romanticism and, like the other, fails to deal with the fact that the speaker is often not presented objectively but is a means of communicating the poet's likes or dislikes, his personal vision.

Both these explanations of Victorian dramatic monologue pivot round a subjective-objective dichotomy. However, the analysis of dramatic monologue as feint in chapter 3 above locates it in neither of these categories; in fact, it hovers teasingly between the poet's 'I' figure and an independent fictional world. The subjective-objective dichotomy is misleading - it is itself a product of Romanticism and one which it is by no means easy to clarify. Browning uses it with diffidence: 'an objective poet, as the phrase now goes'; 'the subjective poet of modern classification' ('Essay on Shelley').

The present study takes the view that Victorian poets adapted dramatic monologue out of the tradition described in the previous chapter. We should therefore look for the changes they introduced. The main one is that Browning especially takes much further the eighteenth-century tendency towards naturalistic and dramatic presentation.

This takes us back to the distinctions that were drawn in the first two chapters. The difference between 'Fra Lippo Lippi' and earlier poems is not in the basic mode of understanding required of the reader. We have seen that the combination of sympathy and judgment occurs in varying proportions in dramatic monologues of all periods, and that a divided consciousness always results from the use of the first person by a speaker who is indicated not to be the poet. Writers of all periods use the form as a way of communicating their views. Nevertheless, Browning's dramatic monologues - not always but often - establish the speaker's individual perspective to a greater extent through a full apparatus of time, place, language and sometimes an auditor. 'I am poor brother Lippo, by your leave!/You need not clap your torches to my face' may be compared with the opening of Wordsworth's 'Lament of Mary Queen of Scots':

> Smile of the Moon! - for so I name
> That silent greeting from above;
> A gentle flash of light that came
> From her whom drooping captives love.

The exclamation is similarly colloquial and immediate, there is a specific setting and the speaker is a named individual. It is not a difference of kind but of degree: Browning's poem is manifestly less declamatory and statuesque, the speaker is more particularized and alive.

Correspondingly, there is a weakening of the sense that a dramatic monologue belongs to a genre such as the epistle or complaint. Earlier poets were less concerned with the peculiar identity of the speaker than his participation in a known form. Usually the title makes the point; sometimes the speaker himself is aware of genre. Daniel's Rosamond refers back to *The Mirror For Magistrates:*

> No Muse suggests the pittie of my case,
> Each penne dooth overpasse my just complaint,
> Whilst others are preferd, though farre more base:
> *Shores* wife is grac'd, and passes for a Saint.

Drayton explains at the start of *England's Heroicall Epistles* that he uses the word 'heroicall' in the same way as Ovid to refer to men 'who for the greatnesse of Mind come neere to Gods'. This is the stature he wishes us to accord his lords and ladies and he stakes his claim by reminding us of Ovid's poem. The ironic reversals of dramatic epistle by Donne, Rochester and Burns depend upon a similar awareness. Even Chaucer's Pardoner and Wife of Bath would probably have been recognized as after the manner of Faux-Semblant and La Vieille in the *Roman de la Rose*.

The impulse to relate these changes to the Romantic movement is surely correct, and we may sketch in briefly the connections. Genre implies a hierarchy and fixity of cultural values and a generalizable quality in human behaviour. In the nineteenth century it no longer seemed possible to sustain it in an unselfconscious manner in the face of the rapid and manifold economic, social and intellectual changes which were taking place. The decay of genre, therefore, is associated with Romantic emphasis upon individual experience. At the same time, the loss of the system of values which had ratified genre, together with the impressive achievements of the biological and physical sciences, led writers (despite fervid assertions of a spiritual dimension in life) increasingly to conceive of the human personality in secular and material terms. Hence the attention to naturalistic detail of individual psychology, of immediate physical and social environment and, above all, of language. We are liable to assume without question that it is by such means that a person is essentially to be identified, whereas earlier writers thought of men more in relation to religious and ethical norms which were perceived as permanent and expressed through the generalizing tendency of established forms.

The changes in dramatic monologue introduced by the Victorians are, therefore, related to large movements of sensibility; indeed, they occur equally in nineteenth-century lyric poetry - for instance in 'Lines composed above Tintern Abbey' and Browning's 'One Word More'. However, they also have special consequences for the uncertain balance between poet and speaker in dramatic monologue. As we remarked in chapter 3, a detailed personality and setting, perhaps including a silent auditor, sets the speaker more firmly apart from the poet and hence tilts the feint towards fiction. Fra Lippo Lippi has a more definite existence than almost any previous dramatic first-person speaker; for many readers his world is so fully established that they are entirely convinced and drawn into it though I believe, as I have argued, that our consciousness of the poet's control of the feint is ultimately irreducible. The first-person mode, by retaining the speaker's claim for existence in the world of the reader, prevents the circle of fiction from closing itself, but the speaker's otherness is nevertheless more sharply asserted.

The question may then be posed in the following form: Why do Victorian poets use dramatic monologue more frequently and for more important poems, and often in such a way as to shift the feint towards the realm of fiction? I shall contend that these developments occur primarily because of a change in attitude to the poet's 'I' figure.

Consider further the Romantic notion of the poet. His personal musings - the more personal the better - were accorded an extraordinary authority; often he was regarded explicitly as a visionary. Tennyson and Browning were influenced by this attitude. Browning said the subjective poet expresses 'Not what man sees, but what God sees - the *Ideas* of Plato, seeds of creation lying burningly on the Divine Hand' ('Essay on Shelley'). Tennyson wrote in an early poem, 'The Poet', 'He saw thro' life and death, thro' good and ill,/ He saw thro' his own soul'. Of *In Memoriam* he declared, '"I" is not always the author speaking of himself, but the voice of the human race speaking thro' him'. Their friends repeatedly urged them to speak out with full bardic authority. Elizabeth Barrett insisted, 'I do not think that, with all that music in you, only your own personality should be dumb, nor that having thought so much and deeply on life and its ends, you should not teach what you have learnt, in the directest and most impressive way, the mask thrown off' (letter of 25 May 1846).

Now, what could be more hampering for a writer than to feel that he must express 'what God sees' or be 'the voice of the human race'? Whenever the poet says 'I' the reader expects a personal truth which is also ultimately a truth about humanity. Truth about oneself, let alone mankind, cannot be encapsulated so plainly within fourteen lines or four hundred.

Earlier writers were not thus inhibited. They could express a range of attitudes without having to feel that they were personally committed to each one. When Donne or Marvell wanted to write about fidelity to one woman he did that; when he wanted to write about seizing sexual pleasure where it offered he did that. The sense of genre - and this was the value of a light disguise like the pastoral convention - enabled him to slip into an appropriate voice and suggest nuances of meaning by setting his treatment against more common uses of the form. In the preface to his *Poems* (1656) Cowley remarks that the poet 'may be in his own practice and disposition a *Philosopher*, nay a *Stoick*, and yet speak sometimes with the softness of an amorous Sappho'. This sounds like Browning's approach, but Cowley is not writing dramatic monologue: the poems he is introducing are all in his own apparent person.

The value of dramatic monologue to Victorian poets, and the reason why they preferred to circumstantiate their speakers strongly, was that this enabled them to evade the inconveniences of the Romantic 'I' whilst at the same time achieving oblique self-expression through the device of the feint. Romantic stress upon the figure of the poet, his visionary capacity, his integrity and sincerity, greatly limited the flexibility of the first-person. The poet felt that when he said 'I' it should really be his true voice; anything else would be a betrayal of his lofty vocation. Only by making it clear that the speaker is *not* 'I' could he extend his tonal range and come indirectly at his theme. Hence dramatic monologue, formerly an occasional device, became invaluable. A greater use of the feint was precipitated by a restriction upon the range of the lyric 'I' figure.

Wordsworth and Coleridge's use of dramatic monologue is instructive. As we have seen, they included complaints among their minor work, but they were embarrassed by their own experiments with naturalistic dramatic monologue. Wordsworth wrote a splendid example in 'The Thorn', where a garrulous and superstitious old man tells the story of a woman who may have lost her mind and murdered her child. He forfeits our sympathy when he twice uses the scandal-monger's ploy of propagating a rumour whilst professing to disbelieve it, and when he pruriently advises the poet to peer into the woman's hut and then, if she's not there, to hasten to view the dreadful spot. The pathos of the story is beyond that overtly stated: the woman suffers also a continual persecution by such foolish neighbours. Wordsworth explained that he had used a 'loquacious narrator' but neither Southey nor Coleridge (nor most later critics) could see the point and Wordsworth lost confidence and deleted the more idiosyncratic speech. Coleridge set out to employ a rustic speaker in 'The Three Graves' but did not finish the poem and felt obliged to explain in a preface, 'The language was intended to be dramatic; that is, suited to the narrator. . . . At all events, it is not presented as Poetry, and it is in no way connected with the Author's judgment concerning Poetic diction'.

Romantic notions of the poet's duty to speak out in noble tones triumphed here but Tennyson and Browning welcomed in dramatic monologue a means of evading the simple sincerity of the Romantic poetic 'I'. This was not a dishonest failure to take responsibility for their views, as has been suggested, but a recognition that truth is complex. (One should always be wary of theories which postulate the blindness of the poet and the shrewdness of the critic.)

Tennyson entitled an early poem 'Supposed Confessions of a second-rate sensitive mind not in unity with itself' not because he had stated his difficulties over religion and wanted to pretend that they were not his - a fruitless ruse since critics always assume, romantically, that they were - but because, although he felt partially thus, he could also see inadequacies in such a position. His poem 'Despair' is spoken by a man who has attempted suicide because he believes the universe to be blind and mechanical. Many passages - *In Memoriam* iii and 'The Two Voices', for example - show that this alarm occurred forcefully at times to Tennyson, but it did not represent his final judgment. The dramatic form of 'Despair' places it in a context with two other attitudes: the auditor is the hell-fire preacher whose doctrine Tennyson believes promotes fatalism, and the speaker has an intuition - which his religious background prevents him from affirming - of a God of love. Tennyson's view emerges in a way which shows that its foundation is essentially intuitive and after due weight has been given to other attitudes whose rationale he well understands.

This kind of strategy is the source of the ambiguity of 'The Lotos-Eaters', where the *Odyssey*, Victorian culture and the whole western tradition suggest that we should disapprove of intoxicated indolence, but imagery, sound and rhythm all tempt the reader into acquiescence. By choosing the dramatic form Tennyson has permitted us not to identify the speakers' words simply with himself. It is his means of saying that he can see the attractions of such inactivity without denying the virtues of perserverance, which he also believed in.

The speakers stand in the same kind of relationship to

Tennyson in 'Locksley Hall' and *Maud*. He denied repeatedly that these poems are autobiographical, although it is known that the theme of thwarted marriage was close to his experience. It is 'the fashion in these days to regard each poem and story as a story of the poet's life', he complained in a note to 'Locksley Hall Sixty Years After', but the relationship is more oblique: 'some event which comes to the poet's knowledge, some hint flashed from another mind, some thought or feeling arising in his own, or some mood coming - he knows not whence or how - may strike a chord from which a poem evolves its life'. It is not that Tennyson disguises his 'true' feelings, any more than a Renaissance lyricist was necessarily expressing such an improbably straightforward emotional state. Nor is he in an ethical limbo where all attitudes are equally worth consideration. He is claiming a flexible and various relationship between inspiration and creation, and the feint is more versatile than the simple sincerity of the Romantic 'I'.

The issue is usefully accessible in the case of Swinburne. When replying publicly to attacks on *Poems and Ballads* (1866) he insisted that 'the book is dramatic, many faced, multifarious; and no utterance of enjoyment or despair, belief or unbelief, can properly be assumed as the assertion of its author's personal feeling or faith' ('Notes on Poems and Reviews'). Privately to W.M. Rossetti he admitted that his poems reflect his opinions, but still denied that they do so simply and directly: 'As to the antitheism of 'Félise' I know of course that *you* know that the verses represent a mood of mind and phase of thought not unfamiliar to me; but I must nevertheless maintain that no reader (*as* a reader) has a right (whatever he may conjecture) to assert that this is *my* faith' (letter of 9 October 1866). The poem represents a 'mood' or 'phase'. The volume is made up of various attitudes endorsed to varying degrees; they are all aspects of Swinburne but none has the authority of a final personal utterance.

At the end of *The Ring and the Book* Browning explains his use of dramatic obliquity. The reader does not like to be told the truth,

> Which truth, by when it reaches him, looks false,
> Seems to be just the thing it would supplant,
> Nor recognizable by whom it left -
> While falsehood would have done the work of truth.
> But Art, - wherein man nowise speaks to men,
> Only to mankind, - Art may tell a truth
> Obliquely, do the thing shall breed the thought,
> Nor wrong the thought, missing the mediate word.

The difficulty Browning identifies is not just the reader's incomprehension. He sees also that truth is not easily stated: it is not 'recognizable by whom it left', the attempt may 'wrong the thought'. He has truths to express but they involve delicate nuances, and dramatic indirection affords opportunity for discrimination and qualification.

Browning is more of a dramatic writer than Tennyson: he has more interest in the thoughts and emotions of others for themselves. Nevertheless, his use of dramatic monologue for oblique self-expression is apparent in the way his speakers return to favourite themes. Consider the opinion which the organist Abt Vogler (in the poem of that name) comes upon whilst improvising, that God will make perfect in an after-life that which is incomplete in earthly experience:

> And what is our failure here but a triumph's evidence
>   For the fulness of the days? Have we withered or agonized?
> Why else was the pause prolonged but that singing might issue
>   thence?
>   Why rushed the discords in but that harmony should be
>   prized?

Browning believed this, but the dramatic method brings other thoughts into play. By making Vogler discover the idea Browning indicates that it is possible to grow towards God's perfection in this earthly life; by setting it at the peak of the organist's creative excitement he implies that the artist has special access to such lofty truths; and by showing (in the succeeding lines) its transience he suggests the fragility of visionary moments but also that there is, for the time being, a satisfactory resting place in 'The C Major of this life'.

Browning uses the same idea in 'Cleon' but here he is more cautious and allows that it does not necessarily sweep all scepticism before it. Cleon (a first-century pagan like Karshish) envisages 'Some future state . . . Unlimited in capability' but his determined secularism leads him to resist Christianity despite the preaching of Paul. In 'Andrea del Sarto' it has a yet more uncertain role, for Andrea's wish for 'In heaven, perhaps, new chances, one more chance' appears to be a further self-deception since he does not envisage altering the conditions that have limited his work on earth. 'A Grammarian's Funeral' is probably Browning's most thoroughly ambiguous poem. An early humanist is being carried to his grave by admiring students; he devoted his whole life to learning, but was that worthwhile? The students say so, but some of their praises sound double-edged: 'This is our master, famous, calm, and dead'; 'Learned, we found him!/Yea, but we found him bald too - eyes like lead'. Yet they justify the grammarian's self-sacrifice with the thought Vogler discovered:

> did he not throw on God,
> (He loves the burthen) -
> God's task to make the heavenly period
> Perfect the earthen?

Here Browning's deep convictions clash, for he believed passionately in devotion to an aim but also that life should be lived to the full.

Browning's attribution of this idea to several speakers enables him to develop, overall, a complex treatment of it. Spenser or Donne might use, say, the Platonic concept of love in various poems in different aspects and with differing degrees of assent. They did not expect any of them to be taken as 'the voice of the human race'. Browning, lacking the traditional flexibility of the first person, seeks the same fluidity, fineness of implication and ultimate breadth of statement by setting up a range of speakers within the teasing form of the feint and according his full support to none of them.

That Browning and Tennyson meant their dramatic monologues to be read as feints - however individual the speakers - may be inferred from the way each poet is instantly recognizable from the style of the poems. A nineteenth-century commentator remarked 'Mr Browning's modes of thought never change as he passes from one point of sight to another; ... the *style* of discourse, the springy, sharp definitions, the acute discriminations, the rapier-like thrusts of logic, are all the poet's own, and used by every one of his characters in succession' (*Browning, The Critical Heritage*, p. 290). Surely this is right and an equivalent description could easily be produced for Tennyson. The naturalistic mode of speech and setting does not - is not meant to - convince the reader. By his intellectual rigour, complicated stanza forms, startling effects of sound and rhythm, contortions and jumps in syntax and manifestly evocative images - all that we recognize as 'Browningese' - Browning stamps the dramatic monologues as *his* poems, just as much as the first-person utterances of Wordsworth or Keats.

The interpretation offered here does not necessarily exclude the others discussed; there is no reason to expect just one explanation. However, I believe Victorian dramatic monologue is primarily a strategic adaptation of the first-person voice. It plays across the subjective-objective dichotomy, calling it into question.

Indeed, it might be argued that a poem like 'My Last Duchess' is less about the Renaissance, marriage, pride, insecurity and aestheticism than about the nature of personality and perception. In my view this would be an exaggeration but *Maud*, by penetrating a strange mind with special intensity over time, and *Amours de Voyage* and *The Ring and the Book* by further multiplying perspectives, move in this direction. The Victorian poets demonstrate dissatisfaction with the subjective 'I' of the Romantics and do not allow the reader to rest in the objective 'I' of an externalized character, and the unstable product which results is passed to the next generation.

7
'So I assumed a double part'

If Victorian dramatic monologue is primarily a strategic response to the Romantic poetic 'I' then we might expect it to come under special pressure in the hands of the poets we term 'Modernist'. Yeats, Pound and Eliot were concerned explicitly with such matters at a time when the culture which had traditionally supported poetry seemed to have reached an extreme of disintegration, and Freudian depth psychology seemed to demand a new way of understanding the human personality. The intensification of the stresses which gave rise to the Victorian monologue made vastly more problematic the assertion of the poetic 'I' and its supposed alternative, the objectively realized character. Eliot wrote in his thesis on the philosophy of F.H. Bradley (completed in 1916), 'Everything, from one point of view, is subjective; and everything, from another point of view, is objective; and there is no *absolute* point of view from which a decision may be pronounced'. This is precisely the stance of the feint.

Modernist dramatic monologue deliberately undermines the naturalistic conception of character. The speaker and his situation hang in an insubstantial void. Attention is concentrated upon moments of intense apprehension which transcend circumstances and perhaps personality; all else is sheared away. Concreteness resides not in a social and physical setting but in brief and evocative images (Pound's monologue 'The Jewel Stairs' Grievance' is only four lines long, though it does have six lines of annotation). Further, we observed that the presence of Tennyson and Browning is felt through their dramatic speakers because of style and their controlling hand, and that they exploit the resulting uncertainty of focus. Modernist poets make a point of intruding explicitly upon their characters so as to prevent the reader from assuming a subjective-objective dichotomy. He must pick his way as best he can through a world of shifting images whilst in doubt of the status of the mind through which they appear to be passing.

The fullest instance is Eliot's 'The Love Song of J. Alfred Prufrock' (1917). The speaker is not located firmly in time and space - he may or may not go out to 'make our visit', and at times he seems to be in the room where 'the women come and go/Talking of Michelangelo'. Finally he says he is at the bottom of the sea. He has many styles of speech: the brutal apprehension of 'restless nights in one-night cheap hotels' is qualified by the evocative but self-consciously extended image of 'The yellow fog that rubs its back upon the window-panes'; this in turn is set against the social manner of 'the taking of a toast and tea' and the colloquial self-deprecation of 'And in short, I was afraid'. Nor can we say simply that all this represents Prufrock's 'stream of consciousness', for Eliot's voice obtrudes and disturbs the fiction. The clipped rhymes, significant line lengths and juxtapositions of tone display Prufrocks's inadequacies just too sharply for self-analysis ('Should I, after tea and cakes and ices,/Have the strength to force the moment to its crisis?'). The epigraph from Dante, borrowings from Laforgue and allusions to Shakespeare, Ecclesiastes, Hesiod and Marvell establish the poem as a literary construct. Moreover, the first line - 'Let us go, then, you and I' - plays strikingly upon the roles of speaker and auditor in traditional dramatic monologue, for there seems to be no third party present. Is Prufrock speaking to his mental image of the lady later referred to? to the reader? to the poet? to another part of himself? Most readers incline to the last answer but in any event our preconceptions about the objective existence of the speaker are openly challenged.

His essay 'The Three Voices of Poetry' (1957) suggests how Eliot derived this disruptive technique from an understanding of the carefully poised relationship between poet and speaker maintained by the Victorians. The 'three voices' are the poet talking to himself, to an audience and within a dramatic character - by the latter he means a voice created by the poet but independent of his own immediate tones and concerns. Eliot thinks it unlikely that the third type of voice will be heard in dramatic monologue because its writer has not the stimulus to detachment which occurs when he is obliged to service a range of characters in a play or novel. Characteristically in dramatic monologue the poet is audible through the speaker: 'In *The Tempest*, it is Caliban who speaks; in "Caliban upon Setebos", it is Browning's voice that we hear, Browning talking aloud through Caliban.' The 'incompleteness of the illusion' is the special quality of the form. Eliot recognizes Caliban as a feint, a strategic adaptation of Browning; in his own work he adds a new dimension by making this self-conscious. He thrusts forward the controlling mind of the poet so that the relationship between author and speaker becomes a theme of the poem.

Yeats' awareness of these issues is already apparent in his poems of the 1890s. 'The Fiddler of Dooney', 'The Song of the Wandering Aengus', 'The Meditation of the Old Fisherman' and 'The Lamentation of the Old Pensioner' make little pretence at realistic characterization:

> There's not a woman turns her face
> Upon a broken tree,
> And yet the beauties that I loved
> Are in my memory;
> I spit into the face of Time
> That has transfigured me.   ('The Old Pensioner')

The love of beauty, the sense of inadequacy before it and the defiant gesture are transparently Yeatsian and he does not try seriously to disguise it. The persona is a temporary convenience and a reminder that the relationship between poet and speaker cannot be taken for granted.

Next Yeats began to use systematically two personae - Michael Robartes, who is mystical and daring, and Owen Aherne who is pious and conventional. Again the relationship with Yeats' own preoccupations is apparent - subsequently he half accepted responsibility for some of these poems by giving them strangely depersonalizing titles in the manner of 'He Bids His Beloved Be at Peace'. Between 1900 and 1914 he came to believe that the human personality is actually composed of a series of masks. He developed a theory of the self and the anti-self in which a defining distinction is that one is subjective and the other objective. The Victorians gained a position from which to write by working along the line between these polarities; Yeats, mainly in dialogues, confounded them by locating both within the mind of the poet.

Ezra Pound began writing with an outlook close to Yeats' and a deep respect for Browning. Like the latter, he felt obliged to explain himself. He wrote to William Carlos Williams, 'Remember, of course, that some of the stuff is dramatic and in the character of the person named in the title' (letter of 21 October 1908). Nevertheless, he did not mean that his speakers are simply objective. He declares in 'Histrion' (in *A Lume Spento*, published in 1908) that he actually *is* his characters for an instant:

> 'Tis as in midmost us there glows a sphere
> Translucent, molten gold, that is the 'I'
> And into this some form projects itself:
> Christus, or John, or eke the Florentine;
> And as the clear space is not if a form's
> Imposed thereon,
> So cease we from all being for the time,
> And these, the Masters of the Soul, live on.

The essential self, Pound says, is so delicate that it takes form only when expressing the personality of another. The poetic 'I' is simultaneously the poet and a character.

The monologues written under this persuasion are mostly supposed to be spoken by medieval poets. Pound constructs a language which hovers somewhere between what might be said by the speaker and a self-conscious recreation of the style of the speaker's own poems:

> Towards the Noel that morte saison
> (*Christ make the shepherds' homage dear!*)
> Then when the grey wolves everychone
> Drink of the winds their chill small-beer
> And lap o' the snows food's gueredon
> Then makyth my heart his yule-tide cheer
> (Skoal! with the dregs if the clear be gone!)
> Wining the ghosts of yester-year.
>
> ('Villonaud for this Yule')

One is reminded irresistibly of Ben Jonson's remark that Spenser, in his affectation of archaisms, writ no language. The poem is located in a limbo between François Villon and Pound's manifest contrivance.

'Cino' is set by its subtitle in 'Italian Campagna 1309, the open road' and opens with the Browningesque,

> Bah! I have sung women in three cities,
> But it is all the same;
> And I will sing of the sun.

Cino is in fact quite willing to speak of his love-life and does so in naturalistic manner. However, his song of the sun is plainly Pound's pastiche:

> 'Pollo Phoibee, old tin pan, you
> Glory to Zeus' aegis-day,
> Shield o' steel-blue, th' heaven o'er us
> Hath for boss thy lustre gay!

Yet the poem closes in another vein:

> I will sing of the white birds
> In the blue waters of heaven,
> The clouds that are spray to its sea.

The poem finds it way back, as it were, from dramatic personality to a pure lyric impulse which ancient and modern poet may share. By transcending the style he has fashioned for Cino, Pound breaks down differences of space and time. The external other and the perceiving consciousness are made to seem elusive and the boundary between them indefinite.

Explicit dissatisfaction with the assertion of the Romantic 'I' and its obverse postulation, the objective character, is taken to an extreme by Pound in *Hugh Selwyn Mauberley* (1919-20). Here he moves freely between quotation, translation, the first and third persons and dramatic monologue, refusing to allow the reader to rest in any one interpretation of the status of the speaker (critics still disagree about who speaks when). Most of the first part of the sequence appears to be a dramatic monologue spoken by a poet named Mauberley, but the first piece is an epitaph written in the third person. Its title - 'E.P. Ode pour l'Election de son Sepulcre' - links the protagonist with Pound but at the same time sets him up as a literary device by alluding to the sixteenth-century poet Ronsard who wrote a similarly titled poem about himself. Pound-Mauberley's trip through literary London is made wilfully obscure by private references, allusions to foreign literatures and abrupt transitions. The second part turns Mauberley into an artist and offers a more subjective and self-critical revision of the themes of the first part.

The Waste Land is Eliot's largest exercise in the simultaneous disintegration of the personalities of poet and characters. The barmaid in 'A Game of Chess' is fully individualized in language, attitudes and location, though echoes of Ophelia finally assert her literary status, but the others fade in and out of each other. Eliot explained (though of course it explains very little): 'Just as the one-eyed merchant, seller of currants, melts into the Phoenician Sailor, and the latter is not wholly distinct from Ferdinand Prince of Naples, so all the women are one woman, and the two sexes meet in Tiresias'. In traditional dramatic monologue the feint is always flickering - varying with the degree to which the poet sustains the fictional persona or obtrudes his larger knowledge; a poem like 'Cino' exploits this uncertainty systematically; *Mauberley* and *The Waste Land* create from it a whole mode of consciousness.

The goal of all this indirection and determined disconcerting of the reader may be wider than an expression of the Modernist dilemma in a particular poem. Dramatic monologue and allied forms may be employed by the poet, perhaps not altogether intentionally, as provisional languages through which he may gradually develop a first-person voice which does not suffer the disadvantages the Victorians sought to avoid. If the poet can cultivate a poetic 'I' which is sufficiently elusive and impersonal to suggest the mysterious and incalculable nature of the human psyche; which heads off the Romantic assumption that the poet's self may be encapsulated, and truth with it, in a single language act; which possesses an ironical self-awareness but does not inhibit commitment; then he will no longer need dramatic monologue. He will have found his way back to the flexibility of first-person voice enjoyed before the Romantics - though not with the innocence of earlier poets. Dramatic monologue by affording scope for experiment contains within itself the means of its own redundancy.

Eliot already had such a movement in mind in 'Tradition and the Individual Talent' (1919), where he declared that the mind of the mature poet does not have more 'personality' or 'more to say' but is 'a more finely perfected medium in which special, or very varied, feelings are at liberty to enter into new combinations'. Pound commented on the quest for a viable poetic voice in an essay which first appeared in 1914:

> One says 'I am' this, that, or the other, and with the words scarcely uttered one ceases to be that thing. I began this search for the real in a book called *Personae*, casting off, as it were, complete masks of the self in each poem. I continued in a long series of translations, which were but more elaborate masks.
>
> (*Gaudier-Brzeska,* London, 1960, p. 85)

The link here between translation and poems like 'Cino' and 'Villonaud for this Yule' is very interesting. Because the poet admits fully that he *is* translating, first-person translations are perfect feints, though in a contrary manner from dramatic monologue. Now it is the poet's 'I' figure who confessedly is not 'himself': the poet masquerades as his source. Both translation and dramatic monologue afford opportunities to try out other languages as stages towards a personal style.

Some of Pound's translations of Chinese poems are actually of dramatic monologues. They are curiously reminiscent of European modes and show well how he gained in tonal range. 'The River-Merchant's Wife: a Letter' recalls the epistles of love-lorn women which we have derived from Ovid, but unaccustomed social assumptions promote a peculiar mixture of passion and respect:

> At fourteen I married My Lord you.
> I never laughed, being bashful.
> Lowering my head, I looked at the wall.
> Called to, a thousand times, I never looked back.
>
> At fifteen I stopped scowling,
> I desired my dust to be mingled with yours
> For ever and for ever and for ever.
> Why should I climb the look out?

The combination of intimacy and formality is quite unlike any European love language.

Pound remarked, 'Neither can anyone learn English, one can only learn a series of Englishes. Rossetti made his own language. I hadn't in 1910 made a language, I don't mean a language to use, but even a language to think in' (*Literary Essays*, p. 194). However, it may be disputed whether he or Yeats in fact arrived at the entirely flexible voice of pre-Romantic poets. Pound preferred in the *Cantos* a continuing restless experimentation with multiple and shifting personae, sometimes reverting to shrill didacticism. Yeats gained a fuller tone better suited to his personality, but partly by adopting a Romantic bardic stance. His later poems offer a new stylization and self-dramatization; alternatively they use dramatic monologue in a traditional manner to set up spokesmen for the poet's opinions. These comments are not necessarily evaluative: in such matters it may be as well to journey interestingly as to arrive.

In *Four Quartets* (1943) Eliot achieved unity of style whilst comprising the most varied tones. The poem is spoken in the poet's own apparent person but by the use of allusive quotation, pastiche and formal stanzaic sections placed in regular positions any simple relation to Eliot the man is denied. The poetic 'I' is flexible and impersonal, and hence able to regard a theme through a range of tones without being self-cancelling. For the duration of the reading at least we feel that the voice has an authority beyond just that of Eliot himself. In 'Little Gidding' the poet, who is at once in London after an air raid and in Dante's Hell, meets 'a familiar compound ghost':

> So I assumed a double part, and cried
> And heard another's voice cry: 'What! are *you* here?'
>   Although we were not. I was still the same,
> Knowing myself yet being someone other -
> And he a face still forming.

This expresses exactly the relation between the poet and his various poetic selves. As his other self, which is also the literary tradition, tells him, 'last year's words belong to last year's language/And next year's words await another voice'. Yet these are all recognizably voices of the poet: Eliot no longer needs dramatic monologue.

8
Conclusion

The battles of Modernism have been won or no longer seem so important. Subsequent poets have used the approach either of Auden or Dylan Thomas. The latter, perhaps freed by his Celtic background, strode back into the full bardic posture. Auden took advantage of Eliot's work and moved straight to the cultivation of a poetic 'I' so elusive that it can range with ease from the flip to the solemn to the intimate. The feint becomes unnecessary because awareness of further perspectives is always implicit in Auden's protective ironic stance. Neither poet felt the need to make any significant use of dramatic monologue.

Nevertheless, it has proved valuable to a more recent poet, the American Robert Lowell. In his first volume, *Lord Weary's Castle* (1946), it helps him to express his strident rejection of the New England puritan heritage. 'After the Surprising Conversions' and 'Mr Edwards and the Spider' (discussed in chapter 2) satirically expose the attitudes of Calvinist ministers through their own words. In *The Mills of the Kavanaughs* (1951), a volume of dramatic monologues, Lowell partly shares the concern of Pound and Eliot with the nature of the mind. The speakers dwell upon dreams, reveries and madness, exploring in dense language their inner fantasies and secret passions. However, these poems are also close to Browning in that they make considerable efforts to establish character and situation. This seems to be because Lowell is using his speakers in the Victorian manner to deal indirectly with preoccupations - religion, mental stress, sexual infidelity - which are actually his own.

Lowell recognizes the mode of feint; he has remarked, 'I don't believe anybody would think my nun [in 'Mother Marie Therese'] was quite a real person'. Like Eliot and the present study, he finds a similar transparent indirection in Browning's dramatic monologues: 'there's a glaze between what he writes and what really happened, you feel the people are made up' (interview with Frederick Seidel, 1961). The 'glaze' in Lowell's poems consists of violent, allusive and often heavily symbolic imagery, precise formal structures, and syntax which points up these features rather than suggesting spontaneous thought. In 'Mother Marie Therese' an old Canadian nun recalls a mother superior who was drowned:

> O Mother, here our snuffling crones
> And cretins feared you, but I owe you flowers:
> The dead, the sea's dead, has her sorrows, hours
> On end to lie tossing to the east, cold,
> Without bed-fellows, washed and bored and old,
> Bilged by her thoughts, and worked on by the worms,
> Until her fossil convent come to terms
> With the Atlantic. Mother, there is room
> Beyond our harbor. Past its wooden Boom
> Now weak and waterlogged, that Frontenac
> Once diagrammed, she welters on her back.
> The bell-buoy, whom she called the Cardinal,
> Dances upon her.

Lowell is felt through this passage - in the caustic description of the old nuns in the first lines quoted, the grim evocation of the corpse in the sea, the sexual innuendoes, the extension into North American history (Frontenac), the symbolic implication that the convent is a harbour protected by a weakening boom from the violent and uncaring Atlantic with which it must 'come to terms'.

It may be that Lowell, like Eliot, has used dramatic monologue as a route to his own voice. In *Life Studies* (1959) he returned to his own person and his family background with a new ease and coolness of irony. Here he is his own subject in the Romantic manner but there is also an Audenesque holding of the reader off from himself which repudiates any suggestion that he may be entirely known, by the reader or himself. However, Lowell is still experimenting with voices in translation and plays and it may be doubted whether *Life Studies* is a full or final achievement.

For the most part dramatic monologue has returned to occasional use, available when it seems to offer the appropriate form for a particular poem. Sadly, it is often undervalued because of popular prejudices about the Victorians. It is worth recalling the points made in the early part of this study: that dramatic monologue is a specially immediate way of presenting character, that it affords an oblique mode of self-expression and an unusually teasing reading experience.

The reader or poet who questions its continuing validity should consider 'Hawk Roosting' by Ted Hughes and 'Wedding Wind' by Philip Larkin. It is not just that these are fine poems: in each case the poet has been able to extend significantly his accustomed manner. Hughes' hawk conveys disquietingly smug satisfaction:

> My feet are locked upon the rough bark.
> It took the whole of Creation
> To produce my foot, my each feather:
> Now I hold Creation in my foot.

This adds cool dictatorial intention to the descriptive awe with which Hughes regards animals in other early poems. Larkin's female speaker expresses unusually direct sexual experience and lyrical ecstasy:

> Shall I be let to sleep
> Now this perpetual morning shares my bed?
> Can even death dry up
> These new delighted lakes, conclude
> Our kneeling as cattle by all-generous waters?

Fiction and self-expression are equally fundamental to art. By working on the border between them and conceding the entire territory to neither, dramatic monologue invites continuous reconsideration of their claims and capacities. We would be unwise to try to manage without it.

Bibliography

Mainly about dramatic monologue in general

Hazard Adams, *The Contexts of Poetry,* London, 1965.
   Includes a helpful chapter on the form.
Wayne C. Booth, *The Rhetoric of Fiction,* Chicago, 1961.
   An analysis of narrative techniques in fiction.
A. Dwight Culler, 'Monodrama and Dramatic Monologue', *Publications of the Modern Language Association of America,* XC (1975), 366-85.
   Important scholarly light on the non-ironic monologue of sympathetic identification.
K.E. Faas, 'Dramatischer Monolog und Dramatisch-Monologische Versdichtung', *Anglia,* LXXXVII (1969), 338-66.
   Makes clear the difficulty of defining dramatic monologue by a list of formal properties and points out that its use by the Victorians coincides with the idea that the lyric should be a personal statement. Argues that since no poem can properly be taken simply as a statement of the author's, what we have is not two categories - lyric and dramatic monologue - but a range of intensity of relationships between poet and speaker, whether there is an explicit persona or not. Compares Browning's 'My Last Duchess', 'Rabbi Ben Ezra', 'One Word More' and 'The Lost Mistress' from this point of view, regarding 'Rabbi Ben Ezra' as hardly dramatic at all and 'One Word More' as a 'dramatic-monologue poem'. Faas has developed this approach in his book, *Poesie als Psycholgramm, Die Dramatisch-Monologische Versdichtung im Viktorianischen England,* München, 1974.

Benjamin Willis Fuson, *Browning and his English Predecessors in the Dramatic Monologue*, State University of Iowa Humanistic Studies, VIII (1948).

Thorough descriptive catalogue, little real analysis.

Käte Hamburger, *The Logic of Literature*, 2nd edn, trans. Marilynn J. Rose, Bloomington and London, 1973.

Penetrating but difficult discussion of the implications of first- and third-person narrative. Only for very advanced students.

Philip Hobsbaum, 'The Rise of the Dramatic Monologue', *Hudson Review*, XXVIII (1975-6), 227-45.

Relates dramatic monologue to stage conditions. Useful description of some of Browning's followers.

Robert Langbaum, *The Poetry of Experience*, revised edn, Harmondsworth, 1974.

Brilliant and provocative seminal account of the whole topic.

M.W. MacCallum, *The Dramatic Monologue in the Victorian Period*, Proceedings of the British Academy, London, 1925.

Many suggestive points.

Ina Beth Sessions, 'The Dramatic Monologue', *Publications of the Modern Language Association of America*, LXII (1947), 503-16.

The principal attempt at formal classification.

Mainly about individual poets

Richard D. Altick and James F. Loucks, II, *Browning's Roman Murder Story: A Reading of 'The Ring and the Book'*, Chicago, 1968.

Treats the poem in great detail with much valuable material.

Philip Drew, *The Poetry of Browning*, London, 1970.

Original discussion of the form and of many of Browning's monologues. Especially chs 2, 3, 6.

Betty S. Flowers, *Browning and the Modern Tradition*, London, 1976.

Chapter 4 is about 'The Dramatic Method'.

Park Honan, *Browning's Characters,* New Haven, 1961.
Browning's monologues from many aspects. Review of issues of principle in ch. 4 clears the ground.

Roma A. King, Jr, *The Bow and the Lyre,* Ann Arbor, 1957.
Sensitive account of five of Browning's dramatic monologues.

Boyd Litzinger and Donald Smalley (eds), *Browning, The Critical Heritage,* London, 1970.
A mass of material by nineteenth-century critics. See especially items 70, 87, 93, 94, 95, 105, 120, 132, 133, 179, 228, 245.

Michael Mason, 'Browning and the Dramatic Monologue' in *Robert Browning,* ed. Isobel Armstrong, London, 1974.
Takes the form back to first principles; valuable discussion of Browning's 'Porphyria's Lover'.

Mary Rose Sullivan, *Browning's Voices in 'The Ring and the Book',* Toronto, 1969.
Illuminating clarification of Browning's aims and methods.

James R. Kincaid, *Tennyson's Major Poems,* New Haven, 1975.
Lively and perceptive analysis of monologues in chs 3, 6, 7.

Alan Sinfield, 'Tennyson's Imagery', *Neophilologus,* LX (1976), 466-79.
Further development of the view of *Maud* in the present study.

Paul Turner, 'Some Ancient Light on Tennyson's "Oenone", *Journal of English and Germanic Philology,* LXI (1962), 57-72.
Shows the poem to be 'a distillation, not of life, but of literature'.

Isobel Armstrong, *The Major Victorian Poets: Reconsiderations,* London, 1969.
Essays by A.S. Byatt on *Maud,* John Killham and Isobel Armstrong on *The Ring and the Book,* and John Goode on *Amours de Voyage.*

Richard Ellmann, *Yeats, the Man and the Mask,* revised edn, London, 1961.
The poet's struggle with his personality and with poetic form.

Thomas H. Jackson, *The Early Poetry of Ezra Pound,* Cambridge, Mass., 1968.
Much of value on dramatic monologues.

T.S. Eliot, 'The Three Voices of Poetry' in *On Poetry and Poets*, London, 1957.

Includes a stimulating aside about dramatic monologue.

T.S. Eliot (ed.), *Literary Essays of Ezra Pound*, New York, 1954.

Especially the review of *Prufrock*.

Hugh Kenner, *The Invisible Poet: T.S. Eliot*, London, 1960.

Sensitive to the mode of Eliot's early poems.

Thomas Parkinson (ed.), *Robert Lowell*, Twentieth Century Views, Englewood Cliffs, 1968.

Important interview with Lowell and useful essays.

Index